Study Guide
for
Maxfield and Babbie's

Research Methods for

Criminal Justice and Criminology
Second Edition

Martin S. Floss
Hilbert College

West/Wadsworth
I(T)P® An International Thomson Publishing Company

Belmont, CA • Albany, NY • Bonn • Boston • Cincinnati • Detroit • Johannesburg • London
Madrid • Melbourne • Mexico City • New York • Paris • Singapore • Tokyo • Toronto •
Washington

COPYRIGHT © 1998 by Wadsworth Publishing Company
A Division of International Thomson Publishing Inc.
I(T)P® The ITP logo is a registered trademark under license.

Printed in the United States of America
1 2 3 4 5 6 7 8 9 10

For more information, contact Wadsworth Publishing Company, 10 Davis Drive, Belmont, CA 94002, or
electronically at http://www.thomson.com/wadsworth.html

International Thomson Publishing Europe
Berkshire House 168-173
High Holborn
London, WC1V 7AA, England

International Thomson Editores
Campos Eliseos 385, Piso 7
Col. Polanco
11560 México D.F. México

Thomas Nelson Australia
102 Dodds Street
South Melbourne 3205
Victoria, Australia

International Thomson Publishing Asia
221 Henderson Road
#05-10 Henderson Building
Singapore 0315

Nelson Canada
1120 Birchmount Road
Scarborough, Ontario
Canada M1K 5G4

International Thomson Publishing Japan
Hirakawacho Kyowa Building, 3F
2-2-1 Hirakawacho
Chiyoda-ku, Tokyo 102, Japan

International Thomson Publishing GmbH
Strasse 418
53227 Bonn, Germany

International Thomson Publishing Königswinterer
Southern Africa
Building 18, Constantia Park
240 Old Pretoria Road
Halfway House, 1685 South Africa

Print Buyer: Stacey Weinberger

ISBN 0-534-52165-7

Table of Contents

**Criminal Justice Resource Center on the Internet is located at
http://www.wadsworth.com/cj.html**

Preface

This is the Study Guide for *Research Methods for Criminal Justice and Criminology*, Second Edition by Michael Maxfield and Earl Babbie. The guide is designed to help students learn the material presented in this text and review the material for upcoming exams. The exercises in this guide highlight the important terms and concepts discussed in the text and provide a variety of sample test questions intended to evaluate knowledge of the material.

THIS GUIDE SHOULD NOT BE USED AS A SUBSTITUTE FOR READING THE CHAPTER. It is designed to be used only as a supplement to the text. The guide is most effective when used to review the information presented in the textbook, and to test one's knowledge and understanding of the material.

Using the Study Guide

Each chapter contains several components intended to aid the students' learning and understanding of the reading. A brief description of each component and suggestions for its use follows:

<u>Chapter Outline</u> - The chapter outline is a detailed sketch of the entire chapter. Students should <u>not</u> use the outline as a substitute for reading the text itself. In fact, many sentences within the chapter outline's have been partially omitted. It is recommended that students read the supplied outline <u>before</u> beginning the chapter. After reading the textbook, students should return to the Chapter Outline, locate all incomplete sentences (labeled with ❶ ❷ ❸), and complete the missing information: The information can be found in the textbook. Once completed, the student will have covered the information three times, and will have completed a detailed outline which should be used when reviewing for examinations.

<u>Key Names and Terms</u> - This section provides a list of the most important concepts, theories, and theorists discussed in the chapter. Students should be able to define each term, explain each theory, and identify the significant contributions of each individual.

<u>Multiple Choice Questions</u> - In this section, students should choose the <u>best</u> answer to the question. These questions are very similar, though not identical, to questions that may appear on exams and provide an excellent review of the chapter material. These questions provide the most effective review when students attempt to answer all of them. Students can use these questions to assess which areas they have mastered and which areas need additional study.

<u>True/False Questions</u> - This section provides further review of questions similar to those found on common exams.

<u>Essay Questions</u> - These questions often require a detailed, thoughtful, and organized response. The answers to these questions are not always found directly in the text and often require students to apply and synthesize (combine two or more ideas to produce a third, and new, thought) a practical response to difficult problems found within the criminal justice system. Again, students should practice writing complete, concise, and well-organized responses. Be sure to completely address <u>all</u> sections of each question and focus on what is being asked--do not add irrelevant information.

Helpful Study Hints

<u>Use the Study Guide</u> - use the Study Guide to help study, review, and test yourself. The questions included in the guide are similar to those that may appear on an exam; therefore, the guide can provide a good assessment of how well you might fare on a test. Use the guide to determine which parts of the text you understand and which still need some additional review.

<u>Complete the reading before class</u> - It is always best to go to class as prepared as possible, which includes reading the assigned material <u>before</u> going to class.

<u>Understand the chart</u> - Be sure to read and understand any charts, inserts, graphs, or other highlighted materials in the chapter. These segments are intended to illustrate points discussed in the test and can be helpful in clarifying areas that you find unclear.

<u>Take notes on the readings</u> - Do not simply read the chapter from beginning to end without pausing or taking notes. After completing the chapter outline, compare your notes with those found in the outline. If your notes are deficient in some areas, return to the textbook and review those deficient areas.

<u>Participate in class</u> - Students often find it difficult to participate in class, especially if the class is a large lecture class; however, this aspect of the learning experience in invaluable. Try to participate in any way possible--ask questions, answer questions, participate in an ongoing discussion, or raise an issue for discussion.

<u>Go see your instructor</u> - If at all possible, take time to talk with your instructor one-on-one. Make use of his or her office hours or make an appointment if necessary. Instructors can help you clarify points in your notes or explain the reading, and they can provide additional information that may prove useful.

<u>Study time</u> - Do not wait until the last minute to begin studying for a test! It is much more effective to study the material just a little every day than to try to manage it all in one sitting. If at all possible, spend around an hour every day reviewing the lectures and readings. This study method provides more time to reinforce the material, to make connections with other areas, and to more fully understand the issues. This method decreases memorization and increases understanding.

<u>Take pride in your work</u> - Sloppy work reflects on the quality of the work, and will not help you or your grade. An excellent paper that is littered with typing errors, misspelled words, and grammatical mistakes will get a low grade. To avoid these problems, proofread your work before turning it in or have others proofread it for you. Check for any typographical errors, misspelled words, or grammatical mistakes. Try to ensure that your writing is clear and to the point. Eliminate any extra words, rearrange unclear sentences, use small words when they are appropriate, and do not plagiarize other sources of information (use the appropriate citation method). All of these things will improve the overall quality of your work.

<u>Understand the material</u> - Try to avoid simply memorizing the material. Instead, use the essay questions to help you understand the material. Apply what you learn to practical situations, this practice should help you better understand the material. If you truly understand the material, you will remember it longer, reducing study time later. If, after trying rigorously, you still do not understand some piece of material, approach your instructor and ask him or her if they could clarify the issue(s).

I would like to thank Terri L. Watson and Barbara K. Luntz Weiler, who wrote an earlier edition of the instructor's manual and student study guide for Michael Maxfield and Earl Babbie's *Research Methods for Criminal Justice and Criminology*. I would also like to dedicate this manuscript to my wife Kim.

Chapter 1

CRIME, CRIMINAL JUSTICE, AND SCIENTIFIC INQUIRY

Chapter Outline

I. *Introduction*

    A.   This book is about knowing things: Our primary purpose is to assist you in looking at how you know things, not what you know.

    B.   This book is about ❂❂❂   .

II. *Two Realities*

    A.   Ultimately, we live in a world of two realities.

        1.   Part of what we know could be called our *experiential reality*: the things we know ❂❂❂   .

        2.   Another part could be called our ❂❂❂   : things we consider real because we've been told they're real, and everyone else seems to agree they are real.

        3.   The first is a product of our own experience; the second is a product ❂❂❂   .

    B.   **Empirical** research is the production of knowledge based on experience or observation.

    C.   Empirical research is a way of knowing things about crime and criminal justice, and explaining how to conduct empirical research--the purpose of this book.

        1.   There are other ways to conduct research, just as there are other ways of learning things.

        2.   For example, if you are a criminal justice major, many of the other courses you take--say a course on theories of crime and deviance--will contribute to your agreement reality.

    D.   Science offers an approach to both agreement reality and experiential reality. Scientists have ❂❂❂   .

        ◇   In general, an assertion must have both *logical* and *empirical* support: It must make sense, and it must align with observations in the world.

E. *Epistemology* is the science of knowing: *methodology* (a subfield of epistemology) might be called "the science of finding out."

    1. This book is an examination and presentation of criminal justice methodology.

    2. This book considers how social science methods can be used ❂ ❂ ❂ .

III. *Research Producers and Consumers*

A. Why study research methods?

    1. Most criminal justice professionals, especially those in supervisory roles, ❂ ❂ ❂ .

    2. An understanding of research methods can help decision makers critically evaluate such reports, recognizing when methods are properly and improperly applied.

    3. One objective of this book, therefore, is to help future professionals ❂ ❂ ❂ .

B. Maybe you will become a producer of research, in other courses you take or in your job.

    1. Probation officers frequently try out new approaches to client supervision or counseling; determining whether such changes are effective is an example of applied research.

    2. It has become essential in many cities and states to estimate how changes in sentencing policy might affect jail and prison populations.

IV. *Ordinary Human Inquiry*

A. Practically all people exhibit a desire to ❂ ❂ ❂ .
We seem quite willing, moreover, to undertake this task using *causal* and *probabilistic* reasoning.

1.   First, we generally recognize that future circumstances are somehow caused or conditioned by ❂ ❂ ❂   .

2.   Second, people also learn that such patterns of cause and effect are probabilistic in nature: The effects occur more often when the causes occur than when the causes are absent--but not always.

3.   Science makes concepts such as causality and probability more explicit and provides techniques for dealing with them more rigorously than does casual human inquiry.

B.   The attempt to predict is often placed in a context of knowledge and ❂ ❂ ❂

    1.   If you can understand why things are related to one another, why certain regular patterns occur, you can predict even better than if you simply observe and remember those patterns.

    2.   Thus, human inquiry aims at answering both what and why questions, and we pursue these goals by ❂ ❂ ❂   .

V.   *Tradition*

A.   Each of us inherits a culture made up, in part, of firmly accepted knowledge about the workings of the world.

    1.   These are the things that 'everybody knows."

    2.   Tradition, in this sense of the term, has some clear advantages for human inquiry. By accepting what everybody knows, you are spared the overwhelming task of starting from scratch in your search for regularities and understanding.

    3.   Knowledge is ❂ ❂ ❂   , and an inherited body of information and understanding is the jumping-off point for the development of more knowledge.

    4.   At the same time, tradition may be ❂ ❂ ❂   .
If you seek a fresh and different understanding of something that everybody already understands and has always understood, you might be treated as a fool for your efforts.

VI.   *Authority*

A.   Despite the power of tradition, new knowledge appears every day. Like tradition, authority can ❂ ❂ ❂   .

1.   We do well to trust in the judgment of the person who has special training, expertise, and credentials in the matter, especially in the face of contradictory positions on a given question.

2.   At the same time, inquiry can be greatly hindered by the legitimate authority who errs within his or her own special province.

3.   Inquiry is also hindered when we depend on the authority of experts speaking outside their realm of expertise.

B.   Both tradition and authority, then, are double-edged swords in the search for knowledge about the world.

VII.   *Errors in Personal Human Inquiry*

VIII.   *Inaccurate Observation*

◇   The keystone of inquiry is ◒ ◒ ◒   .

1.   We have to know *what* before we can explain ◒ ◒ ◒   .

2.   In contrast to casual human inquiry, scientific observation is a conscious activity.

3.   In many cases, both simple and complex measurement devices help to guard against ◒ ◒ ◒   .

4.   Moreover, they add a degree of precision well beyond the capacity of the unassisted human senses.

IX.   *Overgeneralization*

◇   When we look for patterns among the specific things we observe around us, we often assume that a few similar events are evidence of a general pattern.

1.   Whenever overgeneralization does occur, it can misdirect or impede inquiry.

2.   Criminal justice researchers guard against overgeneralization by committing themselves in advance to a sufficiently large sample of observations, and by being attentive ◒ ◒ ◒

3.   The **replication** of inquiry provides another safeguard. Replication means repeating a study, checking to see if ◒ ◒ ◒   .

X. *Selective Observation*

  ◇ One danger of overgeneralization is that it may lead to ◉ ◉ ◉ .

   1. Once you have concluded that a particular pattern exists and have developed a general understanding of why, you will be tempted to pay attention to future events and situations that correspond with the pattern and ignore those that do not.

   2. A research design will often specify in advance the number and kind of observations to be made as a basis for ◉ ◉ ◉ .

XI. *Illogical Reasoning*

  ◇ People have various ways of handling observations that contradict their conclusions about the way things are.

   ◇ Although all of us sometimes fall into embarrassingly illogical reasoning in day-to-day life, scientists avoid this pitfall by using ◉ ◉ ◉ .

XII. *Ideology and Politics*

  A. Crime is, of course, an important social problem, and there is a great deal of controversy about policies for dealing with crime.

   1. Ideological or political views ◉ ◉ ◉ .

   2. It may be especially difficult for criminal justice professionals to separate ideology and politics from a more detached, scientific approach to the study of crime.

   3. Criminologist Samuel Walker (1994:16) compares ideological bias in criminal justice research to theology: "The basic problem...is that faith triumphs over facts.

  B. Most researchers will have their own beliefs about public policy, including policies directed at crime.

1. The danger lies in allowing such beliefs to distort ❂ ❂ ❂

2. The scientific approach to the study of crime and criminal justice policy guards against, but does not prevent, ideology and theology from coloring the research process.

XIII. *To Err Is Human*

◇ For the most part, social science differs from our casual, day-to-day inquiry in two important respects.

1. First, scientific inquiry is a ❂ ❂ ❂   .
2. Second, social scientific inquiry is more careful than our casual efforts; we are more wary of making mistakes and ❂ ❂ ❂   .

3. Finally, it is important to realize that not only do individuals make every kind of error we've looked at, but social scientists as a group also fall into the pitfalls and stay trapped for long periods of time.

XIV. *The Foundations of Social Science*

A. Science is sometimes characterized as *logico-empirical*: The two pillars of science are (1) logic or rationality and (2) ❂ ❂ ❂   .

1. A scientific understanding of the world must make sense and correspond with ❂ ❂ ❂   .
2. Both of these elements are essential to social science and relate to three major aspects of the overall scientific enterprise: theory, data collection, and data analysis.

B. As a gross generalization, scientific theory deals with the logical aspect of science; data collection deals with the observational aspect, and data analysis looks for ❂ ❂ ❂   .

XV. *Theory, Not Philosophy or Belief*

◇ Social scientific theory has to do with what is, not with ❂ ❂ ❂

1. This means that scientific theory--and, more broadly, science itself--cannot settle debates on ❍ ❍ ❍   .
2. As a practical matter, people are seldom able to agree on criteria for determining issues of value, so science is seldom of any use in settling such debates.
3. One of the biggest problems faced by evaluation researchers is getting people to agree on criteria of ❍ ❍ ❍   .
4. Thus, social science can assist us in knowing only what is and why.
5. It can be used to address the question of what ought to be only when people agree on the criteria for deciding what's better than something else.

XVI. Regularities

A. Ultimately, social scientific theory aims to find patterns of regularity in social life.

1. Lying behind that aim is the fundamental assumption that life is regular, not totally ❍ ❍ ❍   .
2. That assumption, of course, applies to all science.

B. To begin, a vast number of formal norms in society create a considerable degree of regularity.

1. Aside from formal prescriptions, other social norms can be observed that create more regularities (e.g., Teenagers tend to commit more crimes than do persons in middle age).
2. All science is based on the fundamental assumption that regularity exists in what is to be studied, and we have noted that regularities exist in social life.
3. Therefore, logically, social behavior should be susceptible ❍ ❍ ❍   .

XVII. What About Exceptions?

◇ The objection that there are always exceptions to any social regularity is inappropriate.

1. Social regularities represent probabilistic patterns, and a general pattern need not be reflected in 100 percent of the observable cases.
2. This rule applies in the physical sciences as well as in social science.

XVIII. Aggregates, Not Individuals

A. Social scientists, then, primarily study social patterns rather than individual ones.

B. Focusing on **aggregate** patterns rather than on individuals distinguishes the activities of the criminal justice researcher from the daily routines of many criminal justice practitioners.

    1. Social scientific theories deal then, typically, with aggregated, not ❍❍❍

    2. Their purpose is to explain why aggregated patterns of behavior are so regular even when the individuals participating in them may change over time.

XIX. A Variable Language

A. Our most natural attempts at understanding usually take place at the level of the concrete and ❍❍❍

    1. Often people seek a particular, concrete individual.
    2. In social science, however, we go beyond that level of understanding to seek insights into classes or types of individuals.
    3. In other words, we try to identify the concrete individual with some set of similar individuals, and that identification operates on the basis of abstract concepts.

B. One implication of this approach is we'll be able to make sense out of more than one person.

C. The social science involves the study of two kinds of concepts: **variables** and the **attributes** that compose them.

    1. *Attributes* are characteristics or qualities that ❍❍❍
    2. *Variables* on the other hand, are ❍❍❍
    Thus, for example, male and female are attributes, and sex is the variable composed of those two attributes.

D. The relationship between attributes and variables lies at the heart of both description and ❍❍❍ in science.

    ◇ The relationship between attributes and variables is more complicated in the case of explanation and gets to the heart of the variable language of scientific theory.

XX. *Variables and Relationships*

    A.   Theories describe the relationships that might logically be expected among ◐ ◐ ◐ .

        1.   Often, the expectation involves the notion of ◐ ◐ ◐ .
        2.   A person's attributes on one variable are expected to cause, predispose, or encourage a particular attribute on another variable.

    B.   In cause-and-effect terms, the independent variable is the cause, and the dependent variable is the ◐ ◐ ◐ .

    C.   In the construction of a theory, we would derive an expectation regarding the relationship between the two variables based on what we know about each.

        1.   Ultimately, theories are constructed of a variable language.
        2.   It describes the associations that might logically be expected to exist between particular attributes of different variables.

XXI. *Alternative Avenues for Inquiry*

    ◇   There is no one way of doing criminal justice research.

        1.   In fact, much of the power and potential of social science research lies in the many valid approaches it comprises.
        2.   There are three broad and inter-related distinctions that underlie many of the variations of social science research.

XXII. *Idiographic and Nomothetic Explanation*

    A.   All of us go through life explaining things. We do it every day. Sometimes we attempt to explain a ◐ ◐ ◐ .

        1.   This type of causal reasoning goes by the term, idiographic explanation. "Idio-" in this context means unique, separate, peculiar, or distinct, as in the word "idiosyncrasy".
        2.   When we have completed an idiographic explanation, we feel that we fully understand the causes of what happened in this particular instance.
        3.   While parts of the idiographic explanation might apply to other situations, our intention is to ◐ ◐ ◐ .

B.   A second type of causal reasoning is referred to as nomothetic explanation, and is different than idiographic explanation in that nomothetic explanations seek to explain a class of situations or events rather than a single one.

    1.   Moreover, it seeks to explain "efficiently", using ❶ ❷ ❸

    2.   And finally, it settles for partial rather than ❶ ❷ ❸ .

C.   Both the idiographic and the nomothetic approaches to understanding can be useful to you in your daily life. By the same token, both idiographic and nomothetic reasoning are powerful tools for criminal justice research.

    1.   The researcher who seeks an exhaustive understanding of the inner workings of a particular juvenile gang or the rulings of an individual judge is engaging in ❶ ❷ ❸ .

    2.   Sometimes, however, the aim is on more generalized understanding, across a class of events, even though the level of understanding is inevitably more superficial.

D.   Inductive reasoning moves from the ❶ ❷ ❸ .

    ◇   It moves from a set of particular observations to the discovery of a pattern that represents some degree of order among all the varied events under examination.

E.   Deductive reasoning moves from the ❶ ❷ ❸ .

    ◇   It moves from (a) a pattern that might be logically or theoretically expected to (b) observations that test whether the expected pattern actually occurs in the real world.

F.   Deduction begins with *why* and moves to *whether*, while induction moves in just the opposite direction.

XXIII. Quantitative and Qualitative Data

A.   The distinction between quantitative and qualitative data is the distinction between ❶ ❷ ❸ .

1.   All observations are qualitative at the outset.
2.   Quantification often makes our observations more explicit, can make it easier to aggregate and summarize data, and opens up the possibility of statistical analyses, ranging from simple averages to complex formulas and mathematical models.

B.   Quantification involves a focusing of attention and specification of meaning.

C.   On the other hand, qualitative data seem to carry a greater ◐ ◐ ◐

D.   Both qualitative and quantitative methods are useful and ◐ ◐ ◐   .

   ✧   Some research situations and topics are more amenable to qualitative examination, other more amenable to quantification, and still others may require elements of both approaches.

XXIV. *Ethics and Criminal Justice Research*

A.   Ethics is especially important in studying crime and criminal justice, because our interest often centers on human behavior that is illegal.

B.   The foremost ethical rule of social science research is that ◐ ◐ ◐

   1.   Research subjects might be indirectly harmed in ◐ ◐ ◐   .
   2.   Eliminating the potential for harm to subjects is not always possible, but researchers use several general strategies to minimize possible harm.
   3.   Another basic ethical rule of research is that participation should be ◐ ◐ ◐

   4.   You should recognize the importance of ethical issues and the need to consider them throughout the research process.

> *A.* Notice that each alternative avenue for inquiry -- nomothetic and idiographic, inductive and deductive, qualitative and quantitative -- is fundamentally empirical.
>
> B. You may find it helpful to think of criminal justice research as organized around two activities, ❂ ❂ ❂ .
>
> > ◇ Researchers measure aspects of reality and then draw conclusions about the meaning of what they have measured. Whereas all of us are observing all the time, measurement refers to something more deliberate and rigorous.
>
> C. The other key to criminal justice research is ❂ ❂ ❂ .
>
> > 1. Much of interpretation is based on ❂ ❂ ❂ .
> > 2. More generally, however, interpretation is very much dependent on how observations are structured.
>
> D. When you put the pieces together -- measurement, and interpretation -- you are in a position to describe, explain, or ❂ ❂ ❂ .

KEY NAMES AND TERMS

experiential reality	aggregate
agreement reality	attributes
empirical	variables
epistemology	dependent variable
methodology	independent variable
replication	

Multiple Choice Questions

1. Which of the following are advantages of knowledge by tradition?

    a. it allows us to accept "truths" discovered by others.
    b. it spares us from starting over in our search for social regularities.
    c. it allows us to possess cumulative knowledge.
    d. all of the above are advantages.

2. According to the text, the "Kansas City Preventative Patrol Experiment" was an example of

    a. an attack on routine law enforcement practices.
    b. how police could prevent crime.
    c. the importance of good police practice.
    d. how traditional beliefs could be misleading.

3. Traditional beliefs about police patrol effectiveness, response time, and detective work are examples of

    a. experiential reality.
    b. agreement reality.
    c. conservatism.
    d. effectiveness studies.

4. Human inquiry generally involves

    a. systematic observation and empirical testing.
    b. hypothesis testing.
    c. causal and probabilistic reasoning.
    d. statistical analysis.

5. Being Latino is an attribute of which variable?

    a. speaking Latin.
    b. machismo.
    c. religion.
    d. ethnicity.

6. What is ex post facto hypothesizing?

    a. an integral part of the social scientific process.
    b. hypothesizing before data is collected.
    c. explanation after data is analyzed.
    d. illogical reasoning.

7. Errors in human inquiry include

    a. overgeneralization and ideology.
    b. selective observation and inaccurate observation.
    c. premature closure of inquiry and ex post facto hypothesizing.
    d. all of the above are errors in human inquiry.

8. Social scientific theory

    a. addresses what exists in the world.
    b. is the same as philosophy and belief.
    c. focuses on the logical and persistent regularities in social life.
    d. only a and c are true of social scientific theory.

9. What are the fundamental elements of social science?

    a. theory, variables, observation.
    b. philosophy, research methods, replication.
    c. research methods, statistics, ideology.
    d. theory, research methods, statistics.

10. A Federal research agency decides to cut funding for DWI studies because the topic is believed to be understood. What error in human inquiry does this example illustrate?

    a. overgeneralization
    b. inaccurate observation
    c. selective observation
    d. premature closure of inquiry

11. A reporter interviews three students and concludes that there is a campus-wide fear of violent crime. This reporter has fallen prey to the error of

    a. ego involvement in understanding
    b. overgeneralization
    c. ex post facto hypothesizing
    d. ideological bias

12. Maxfield and Babbie state that "we live in a world of two realities":

    a. tradition and authority
    b. experiential and agreement
    c. experiential and logical
    d. agreement and tradition

13. Researchers can guard against overgeneralization through

    a. probabilistic reasoning
    b. replication
    c. ex post facto hypothesizing
    d. selective observation

14. A skillful burglar takes a vacation after a string of successful lootings, for fear that her luck will run out. This criminal has fallen prey to the error of

    a. illogical reasoning.
    b. selective observation
    c. overgeneralization
    d. premature closure of inquiry

15. A staunch advocate of the death penalty dismisses all research that suggests racial bias or a lack of deterrence. Which error in human inquiry does this person make?

    a. ego involvement in understanding
    b. ideological bias
    c. inaccurate observation
    d. illogical reasoning

16. A renowned criminologist refuses to consider any research findings that fail to support the theory that made him famous. This is an example of

    a. illogical reasoning
    b. ex post facto hypothesizing
    c. agreement reality
    d. ego involvement in understanding

17. According to Maxfield and Babbie, the "two pillars of science" are

    a. logic and observation
    b. theory and statistics
    c. tradition and authority
    d. criminology and criminal justice

18. A researcher asks respondents to indicate which of the following drugs they have used: marijuana, inhalants, cocaine, hallucinogens, heroin. These categories of drug use are considered

    a. variables
    b. attributes
    c. social regularities
    d. aggregates

19. "Everybody knows that prison is a punishing experience!" What source of knowledge does this statement reflect?

    a. tradition
    b. experiential reality
    c. empirical research
    d. causal reasoning

20. Social scientific theory focuses on the probabilistic patterns in social life called

    a. variables
    b. social observations
    c. social regularities
    d. agreement reality

True/False Questions

1. Social scientific theory is the same as philosophy or belief.

    a. true
    b. false

2. "Male" is an attribute of the variable 'Sex."

    a. true
    b. false

3. "African-American," "Asian" and "White" are variables of race.

    a. true
    b. false

4. The scientific study of crime prevents ideological and political beliefs from influencing the research process.

   a. true
   b. false

5. The public nature of science helps to prevent illogical reasoning

   a. true
   b. false

Essay Questions

1. What is the difference between tradition and authority? Briefly give an example of each and explain your choices.

2. Using the Kansas City Preventive Patrol Experiment, describe the value of criminal justice research. Continue by describing the errors in personal human inquiry (i.e., inaccurate observation, overgeneralization, selective observation, illogical reasoning, as well as the impact of ideology and politics) and how they can cause society to move in unproductive ways.

Chapter 2

THEORY AND CRIMINAL JUSTICE RESEARCH

Chapter Outline

I. *Introduction*

    A.   One of the livelier academic debates of recent years has concerned the scientific status of disciplines gathered under the heading of social sciences. The movement toward social science has represented a greater emphasis on systematic explanation where the previous emphasis was on ⦿ ⦿ ⦿   .

    B.   This book is grounded in the position that human social behavior can be subjected to scientific study as legitimately as can the physicist's atoms, the biologist's cells, and so forth.

        1.   The study of crime and criminal justice concentrates on particular types of human behavior and is, therefore, no less subject to scientific study.

        2.   This chapter describes the overall logic of social scientific inquiry as it applies to ⦿ ⦿ ⦿   .

II. *The Traditional Model of Science*

    A.   There are three main elements in the traditional model of science which are typically presented in a chronological order of execution.

        1.   Theory
        2.   ⦿ ⦿ ⦿
        3.   observation

    B.   **Theory**—According to the traditional model of science, the scientist begins with an interest in some aspect of the real world.

    C.   **Operationalization**—Operationalization is simply the specification of the steps, procedures, or operations that you will go through in actually identifying and ⦿ ⦿ ⦿   .

        ✧   Operationalization involves deciding how to measure things like crime, social disorganization, and cultural background.

D. **Observation**—The final step in the traditional model of science involves actual observation--looking at the world and making measurements of what is seen.

   1. Having developed theoretical expectations and having created a strategy for looking, all that remains is to ❂ ❂ ❂   .
   2. Sometimes this step involves conducting experiments, sometimes interviewing people, sometimes visiting what you're interested in and watching it.
   3. Sometimes the observations are structured around the testing of specific hypotheses; sometimes the inquiry is less structured.

E. Figure 2-1 provides a schematic diagram of the traditional model of scientific inquiry.

   1. We see the researcher beginning with an interest in something or an idea about it.
   2. Next comes the development of a ❂ ❂ ❂   .
   3. The theoretical considerations result in a hypothesis, or an expectation about the way things ought to be in the world if the theoretical expectations are correct.
   4. In the operationalization process, general concepts are translated into ❂ ❂ ❂   .
   5. This operationalization process results in the formation of ❂ ❂ ❂   .
   6. Observations aimed at finding out are part of what is typically called **hypothesis testing**.

III. *Two Logical Systems*

   A. The traditional model of science uses what is called *deductive logic* which is contrasted with ❂ ❂ ❂   .

   B. Logicians distinguish between inductive reasoning (from particular instances to general principles, from facts to theories) and deductive reasoning (from the general to the particular, applying a theory to a particular case). In induction one starts from observed data and develops a generalization which explains the relationships between the objects observed. On the other hand, in deductive reasoning one starts from some general law and applies it to a particular instance. (W.I.B. Beveridge 1950:113).

   C. Often, social scientists begin constructing a theory by observing aspects of social life, seeking to discover patterns that ❂ ❂ ❂   .

1. Barney Glaser and Anselm Strauss (1967) coined the term ◐◐◐ in reference to this inductive method of theory construction.
2. Field research--the direct observation of events in progress--is frequently used to develop theories through observation.
3. Or survey research may reveal patterns of attitudes that suggest particular ◐◐◐ .

D. **Inductive Theory and Justice Policy**—Consider a different way of looking at inductive theory building, suggested by Barbara Hart: "Practitioners engage in theory building as they ◐◐◐ ."

E. In summary, the scientific norm of logical reasoning provides a bridge between theory and research--a two-way bridge.

1. Scientific inquiry in practice typically involves an alternation between ◐◐◐ .
2. During the deductive phase, we reason *toward* observations
3. During the inductive phase, we reason *from* observations.
4. In practice, both deduction and induction are routes to the construction of social theories.

IV. *Terms Used in Theory Construction*

A. **Objectivity and Subjectivity**—Objective is typically defined as "independent of mind," but our awareness of what might objectively exist comes to us through our minds.

◇ As a working principle, we substitute **intersubjective agreement for objectivity**: If several of us agree that some thing exists, we treat that thing as though it had objective existence.

B. **Observation**—The "experience" of whatever may or may not really exist typically refers to the ◐◐◐ .

1. In the case of social research, this is typically limited to seeing, hearing, and--less commonly--touching.
2. The term *observation* is generally used in reference to such information gathering.

C. **Fact**—Although the notion of a *fact* is as complex for philosophers as the notion of reality, it is generally used in the context of social scientific research to ◐◐◐ .

20

D. **Law**—Abraham Kaplan (1964:91) defines laws as universal generalizations about ❂❂❂ .

   1. Laws in science must be truly universal, however, and not merely accidental patterns found among a specific set of facts.
   2. Laws are sometimes also called *principles* and are important statements about what is so.
   3. Also, laws in and of themselves do not explain anything. They just summarize ❂❂❂ .

E. **Theory**—A theory is a systematic explanation for the observed facts and laws that relate to a particular aspect of life.

   1. Kenneth Hoover (1992:34) defines theory as "a set of related propositions that suggest why events occur in the manner that they do."
   2. Jonathan Turner (1974:3) has examined several elements of theory: concepts, ❂❂❂ , .

F. **Concepts**—Turner (1974:5) calls concepts the "basic building blocks of theory."

   ◇ They are abstract elements representing classes of phenomena within the field of study.

G. **Variables**—A *variable* is a concept's ❂❂❂ .

   1. Where concepts are in the domain of theory, variables can be observed and can take different values--they ❂❂❂ .
   2. Thus, variables require more specificity than concepts.

H. **Statements**—A theory comprises several types of *statements*.

   1. One type of statement is the *axiom*, a fundamental assertion--taken to be true-- on which the ❂❂❂ .
   2. *Propositions* are a another type of statement: conclusions drawn about the relationships among concepts, based on the logical interrelationships among the axioms.
   3. To clarify, an axiom is an assumption about reality, while a proposition ❂❂❂ .

I. **Hypotheses**—*Hypotheses* are specified expectations about empirical reality, derived from ❂❂❂ .

J.   **Paradigm**—No one ever starts out with a completely clean slate to create a theory. A *paradigm* is a fundamental model or scheme that ◑ ◑ ◑

V.   *Theory in Criminal Justice*

◇   Because criminal justice draws on several disciplines--such as sociology, economics, geography, political science, psychology, anthropology, and biology-- different paradigms, or frames of reference, have influenced criminal justice theory, research, and policy.

VI.   *Policy Responses*

A.   Each of the disciplines mentioned above has also influenced studies of how government officials and people in general respond to crime as a policy problem.

B.   Throughout U.S. history, different paradigms associated with punishment come in and go out of fashion. Rehabilitation, retribution, and incapacitation are paradigms in that they represent ◑ ◑ ◑

VII.   *Theory, Research, and Public Policy*

A.   Because crime is an important social problem, rather than simply a social artifact of interest to researchers, much research in criminal justice is closely linked ◑ ◑ ◑

    1.   Research on criminal justice policy is an example of *applied research*-- research results are applied to specific questions about how government officials and the general public should respond to crime.
    2.   Criminal justice theory is just as important in structuring applied research questions as it is in ◑ ◑ ◑

B.   Theory and criminal justice policy are linked in two ways.

    1.   First, as we have seen, theory is used to guide basic research. Results from basic research may suggest ◑ ◑ ◑
    2.   Earlier in this chapter, we said that hypotheses are specified expectations about empirical reality. This statement is also true of policy programs: they are specified expectations about what empirical reality will result from some specific policy action.

22

C. So theory, research, and policy are related in two similar ways:

    1. theory structures research, which in turn is consulted to develop policy.
    2. policies take the form of if-then statements, which implies that they are ❂ ❂ ❂   .
    3. The second way theory is linked to policy forms the basis for evaluation research--studies that assess whether or not some program is achieving its ❂ ❂ ❂   .

VIII. *Ecological Theories of Crime and Crime Prevention Policy*

A. In his introduction to a collection of case studies on situational crime prevention, Ronald Clarke (1992) describes how this approach to criminal justice policy evolved from more general ecological theories of crime.

B. Throughout this chapter, we have seen various aspects of the links between theory and research in criminal justice inquiry.

    1. In the deductive model, research is used to ❂ ❂ ❂   .
    2. And in the inductive model, theories are developed from ❂ ❂ ❂   .

C. The ground we've covered in this section should make you even more aware that there is no simple cookbook recipe for conducting criminal justice research.

    1. It is far more open-ended than the traditional view of science would suggest.
    2. Ultimately, science rests on two pillars: logic and ❂ ❂ ❂   .

KEY NAMES AND TERMS

theory	variables
operationalization	statements
observation	axiom
hypothesis testing	propositions
deductive logic	hypotheses
inductive logic	paradigm
principles	applied research

Multiple Choice Questions

1. Deductive theory construction includes which of the following?

    a. variables.
    b. hypotheses.
    c. ex post facto reasoning.
    d. a and b only.

2. Theory developed from results of empirical analysis refers to the

    a. deductive method.
    b. inductive method.
    c. productive method.
    d. pathological method.

3. Criminal justice theory is primarily concerned with explaining

    a. how the justice system works.
    b. law breaking behavior and responses to that behavior
    c. the cycle of justice.
    d. the relationship between the police and citizens.

4. You are sitting at a desk. This is an example of

    a. subjectivity.
    b. outersubjectivity.
    c. objectivity.
    d. intersubjectivity.

5. Measurable expectations derived from theory are

    a. paradigms
    b. facts.
    c. hypotheses.
    d. variables.

6. The three main elements in the traditional model of science are

    a. hypotheses, theory, and inductive logic.
    b. theory, operationalization, and observation.
    c. crime, analysis, and statistics.
    d. conceptualization, paradigm, and subjectivity.

7.	Which one of the following statement is not characteristic of paradigms?

　　a.	Paradigms influence the type of variables one is likely to examine.
　　b.	Paradigms are very structured and precise.
　　c.	Paradigms affect theory construction.
　　d.	Paradigms can affect policy.

8.	"The use of community policing in a city is expected to reduce the rate of violent crime."
This is an example of a

　　a.	variable.
　　b.	concept.
　　c.	paradigm.
　　d.	hypothesis.

9.	Professor Review observes a number of citizen-police interactions and tentatively concludes that police are more likely to arrest belligerent suspects than more cooperative suspects. This professor has used

　　a.	inductive logic.
　　b.	evaluation research.
　　c.	deductive logic.
　　d.	conceptualization.

10.	Intersubjective agreement refers to

　　a.	a high rate of agreement among subjects in a study.
　　b.	something that is treated as subjective if independent observers agree that it is a matter of individual judgment.
　　c.	something that is treated as though it had objective existence if independent observers agree that it exists.
　　d.	agreement among independent observers that something has been proved to be real.

11.	The following _____ are relevant to social disorganization theory: disorganization, transition zones, and delinquency.

　　a.	observations
　　b.	concepts
　　c.	deductions
　　d.	principles

12. Consider the statement: "Everyone values their freedom." This is an illustration of

    a.   a paradigm
    b.   a law
    c.   an axiom
    d.   a proposition

13. A researcher administers a job satisfaction survey to a group of police officers. The results indicate that officers will be more satisfied with their jobs if they are given greater decision-making power. The findings are used to enact changes in policy so that police officers have a greater say in how their jobs will be done. This is an illustration of

    a.   operationalization
    b.   paradigm shift
    c.   situational crime prevention
    d.   applied research

14. The same researcher later administers a second job satisfaction survey to assess if the policy change described above actually helped to increase police job satisfaction. This is an illustration of

    a.   ex post facto hypothesizing
    b.   evaluation research
    c.   inductive reasoning
    d.   theory construction

15. A student feels that criminal justice research methods is the most enjoyable class he ever had. This is an example of

    a.   objectivity
    b.   a fact
    c.   intersubjectivity
    d.   subjectivity

True/False Questions

1. There is an indirect relationship between theory and policy development.

    a.   true
    b.   false

2. The scientific study of human behavior is inherently different from the study of a physicist's atom, or the biologist's cell, etc.. The study of human behavior cannot be compared to research completed in the natural sciences.

    a.   true
    b.   false

3. Operationalization is the specification of the steps, procedures, or operations that will be used to identify and meausre variables in a particular piece of research.

    a.   true
    b.   false

4. When a reseacher systematically observes reality, in an attempt to find something out, it is referred to as observational testing.

    a.   true
    b.   false

5. Induction involves scientific inquiry that moves from theory towards specific observations.

    a.   true
    b.   false

6. As a working principle, Maxfield and Babbie substitute the concept of intersubjective agreement for objectivity.

    a.   true
    b.   false

7. A law is used in scientific research to mean some pehenomenon that has been observed.

    a.   true
    b.   false

8. A variable is a concept's empirical eounterpart.

    a.   true
    b.   false

9. A paradigm represents a fundamental model or scheme that organizaed ou view of something.

    a.   true
    b.   false

10. It is generally believed by criminal justice researchers that theory and criminal justice policy should not be linked.

   a. true
   b. false

Essay Questions

1. What are the two broad approaches to criminal justice research? Give an example of each.

2. Discuss how criminal justice policy is related to theory. Provide two examples. Finally, state at least one issue that you would be interested in examining, relative to your selected examples. Why? How would a better understanding of your selected issues be relevant for the field of criminal justice?

Chapter 3

CAUSATION AND VALIDITY

I.   *Introduction*

   ◇   One of the chief goals of the scientist, social or other, is to ❂❂❂   .

      1.   Typically, we do that by specifying the causes for the way things are: Some things are caused by other things.
      2.   There are many important, and difficult, questions about causality and validity in criminal justice but our basic approach requires stepping back a bit to consider the larger picture of how we can or cannot assert that some cause actually ❂❂❂   .

II.   *Determinism and Social Science*

   ◇   The deterministic perspective to be discussed now contrasts with a freewill image of human behavior. The fundamental issue is this: Is your behavior the product of your personal willpower or the product of forces and factors in the world that you cannot control and may not even recognize?

III. *Causation in the Natural Sciences*

   ◇   The deterministic model of explanation is in evidence throughout the natural sciences.

      1.   The deterministic model is often applied to human beings as well as to ❂❂❂   .
      2.   We recognize that our free will is limited by certain deterministic constraints.

IV.   *Reasons Have Reasons*

   ◇   Whenever we undertake explanatory social science research -- when we set out to discover the causes of delinquency, for example -- we adopt a model of human behavior that assumes people have ❂❂❂   .

V.   *Determinism in Perspective*

   ◇   As you probably realize, the issue of determinism and freedom is a complex one, which philosophers have debated for thousands of years and will probably debate for thousands more.

1. Our purpose in raising the issue of determinism is to engage you in the question and to alert you to its place in criminal justice research.
2. When people set out to learn the skills of explanatory research, the implicit assumption that human behavior is determined by social and other forces sometimes disturbs them.

B. Let us clarify what is not part of the deterministic model.

1. First, social scientists do not believe all human actions, thoughts, and feelings are determined, nor do they lead their lives as though they believed that.
2. Second, the model does not assume that ❂ ❂ ❂   .
3. Nor does the model assume we are all controlled ❂ ❂ ❂
   .
4. Moreover, the deterministic model lying at the base of explanatory social science does not suggest that we now know all the answers about what causes what or that we ever will.
5. Finally, social science typically operates on the basis of ❂ ❂ ❂
   .
6. You do not necessarily need to believe that human beings are totally determined, nor do you have to lead your life as though you were, but you must be willing to use deterministic logic in looking for explanations when you engage in criminal justice research.

VI. *Idiographic and Nomothetic Models of Explanation*

A. The *idiographic model of explanation*. Attempts explanation by enumerating the many, perhaps unique considerations that lie behind a given action.

1. Of course we never truly exhaust those reasons in practice.
2. Nevertheless, it is important to realize that the idiographic model is employed frequently in many different contexts.

B. The *nomothetic model of explanation* differs from the idiographic model in that it does not involve an ❂ ❂ ❂
   .

1. Rather, the nomothetic model is designed to discover those considerations that are ❂ ❂ ❂   .
2. The nomothetic model of explanation involves isolating those relatively few considerations that will provide a partial explanation for the sentences imposed by many judges or all judges.
3. The goal of the nomothetic model of explanation is to provide the greatest amount of explanation with the fewest number of causal variables to uncover general patterns of cause and effect.

C. The nomothetic model of explanation is inevitably *probabilistic* in its approach to causation.

    1. In the best of all practical worlds, the nomothetic model indicates there is a very high (or very low) probability or likelihood that a given action will occur whenever a limited number of specified considerations are present.

    2. Adding more specified considerations typically increases the degree of explanation, but the basic simplicity of the model calls for balancing a high degree of explanation with a small number of considerations being specified.

VII. *Criteria for Causality*

    A. None of the preceding discussion provides much practical guidance to the discovery of ◑ ◑ ◑ .

        1. Regarding idiographic explanation, Joseph Maxwell (1996:87-88) speaks of the validity of an explanation and says the main criteria are (1) its credibility or believability, and (2) whether alternative explanation ("rival hypotheses") were seriously considered and found wanting.

        2. The first criterion relates to earlier comments about logic as one of the ◑ ◑ ◑ .

        3. The second criterion reminds us of Sherlock Holmes' dictum that when all other possibilities have been eliminated, ◑ ◑ ◑ .

    B. *The first requirement in a causal relationship between two variables is that the cause* ◑ ◑ ◑ .

    C. *The second requirement in a causal relationship is that the two variables be* ◑ ◑ ◑ .

    D. *The third requirement for a causal relationship is that the observed empirical correlation between two variables cannot be explained away as being due to the influence of some third variable that causes both of them.*

VIII.   *Necessary and Sufficient Causes*

♦   Recognizing that virtually all causal relationships in criminal justice are probabilistic is central to understanding other points about cause. Within the probabilistic model, it is useful to distinguish two types of causes: necessary and sufficient causes.

    1.   A *necessary cause* represents a condition that, by and large, must be ◔◔◔   .

    2.   A *sufficient cause*, on the other hand, represents a condition that, if it is present, will pretty much ◔◔◔   .

    3.   The discovery of a necessary and sufficient cause is, of course, the most satisfying outcome in research.

    4.   Unfortunately, we seldom discover causes that are both necessary and sufficient, nor, in practice, are the causes 100 percent necessary or 100 percent sufficient.

IX.   *Molar, Not Micromediational, Causal Statements*

    A.   Cook and Campbell refer to detailed specifications of cause as *micromediational causal statements.*

        1.   A physicist's explanation of why a light comes on presents a micromediational statement about cause.

        2.   Oppositely, typical citizens have what Cook and Campbell call a *molar* understanding of the process: flipping a switch causes a light to come on.

    B.   In criminal justice and other social science research, molar statements about cause can be meaningful even when ◔◔◔   .

        1.   Social science research can productively investigate molar questions about cause.

        2.   You should recognize that this is consistent with our probabilistic approach.

X.   *Errors of Reasoning*

♦   Cause and effect, as we've seen, is essential to scientific explanation: It is also fundamental to our day-to-day lives, and people commonly make errors in their assessment to causation.

XI. Validity and Causal Inference

◇ Paying careful attention to cause-and-effect relationships is ◐ ◐ ◐

       .

1. When we are concerned with whether or not we are correct in inferring that a cause produced some effect, we are concerned with ◐ ◐ ◐
    .

2. Cook and Campbell (1979:37) go on to note that *approximation* is an important word, since one can never be absolutely certain about cause.

3. When we consider whether or not our cause-and-effect statements are true, we consider whether or not they are valid.

4. Cook and Campbell describe a number of different threats to the validity of causal inference, reasons why we might ◐ ◐ ◐
      .

XII. Statistical Conclusion Validity

◇ Statistical conclusion validity refers to our ability to determine whether a change in the suspected cause is statistically associated with ◐ ◐ ◐
     .

1. This corresponds with one of the first questions asked by researchers: Are two variables ◐ ◐ ◐
                           ?

2. However, there may be some technical reasons why we cannot find covariation between phenomena such as drug use and crime. Perhaps we do not have good measures of either the cause of the effect.

3. Another common threat to statistical conclusion validity is basing conclusions on ◐ ◐ ◐
        .

4. Threats to statistical conclusion validity can have the opposite effect of suggesting that covariation is present when in fact there is no cause-and-effect relationship.

XIII. Internal Validity

◇ Internal validity threats also challenge causal statements that are based on the observed relationship.

1. However, while statistical conclusion threats are most often due to random error internal validity problems have their source ◐ ◐ ◐
     .

2. Threats to the internal validity of a proposed causal relationship between two indicators usually arise from the effects of some third variable.

XIV. *Construct Validity*

      ◇   Construct validity is concerned with how well an observed relationship between variables represents the underlying causal process of interest.

            1.   In a sense, construct validity refers to generalizing from what we observe and measure to the real-world things in which we are interested.

            2.   Construct validity is frequently a problem in applied studies, where researchers may ◐◐◐

XV. *External Validity*

      A.   Do research findings about cause and effect apply equally to different cities, neighborhoods, and populations. In a general sense, external validity is concerned with whether research findings from one study can be reproduced in another study, often under different conditions.

            ◇   The tool of replication is used to check on ◐◐◐

      B.   External validity may also refer to the correspondence between basic research under controlled conditions and the real-world application of research findings.

            ◇   Because crime problems and criminal justice responses can vary so much from city to city, or state to state, researchers and public officials are often especially interested in external validity.

XVI. *Validity and Causal Inference Summarized*

      ◇   The four types of validity threats can be grouped into two categories: bias and ◐◐◐

            1.   Internal and statistical conclusion validity threats refer to systematic and nonsystematic bias, respectively.

            2.   Failing to consider the more general cause-and-effect constructs operating in an observed cause-and-effect relationship means that research findings cannot be generalized to real-world behaviors and conditions.

            3.   And a cause-and-effect relationship observed in one setting or at one time may not operate in the same way in a ◐◐◐

XVII. *Does Drug Use Cause Crime?*

      A.   Both construct and external validity are concerned with ◐◐◐

B.   The issue of external validity comes into sharper focus when we shift from basic research that seeks to uncover fundamental causal relationships to criminal justice policy.

XVIII. *Linking Measurement and Association*

◇   As we have seen, one of the key elements determining causation in science is an empirical correlations between the cause and the effect.

1.   All too often, however, the process of measuring variables is seen as separate from that of determining the associations between variables.
2.   This view is incorrect, or at the very least misleading

XIX   *The Traditional Deductive Model*

A.   **Theory Construction**—Faced with an aspect of the natural or social world that interests him or her, the scientist creates an abstract deductive theory to describe it.

B.   **Derivation of Theoretical Hypotheses**—The scientist derives hypotheses relating to the various concepts composing the theory.

C.   **Operationalization of Concepts**—The next step is the specification of empirical indicators to represent the theoretical concepts.

1.   The empirical indicators must be ❂ ❂ ❂
2.   The effect of operationalization is to convert the theoretical hypothesis into an ❂ ❂ ❂

D.   **Collection of Empirical Data**—Based on the operationalization of theoretical concepts, researchers collect data relating to the ❂ ❂ ❂   .

E.   **Empirical Testing of Hypotheses**—Once the data have been collected, the final step is the ❂ ❂ ❂   .

◇   The confirmation or disconfirmation of the empirical hypothesis is then used for purposes of accepting or rejecting the ❂ ❂ ❂   .

F.   Although this traditional image of scientific research can be a useful model for you to have in mind, it tends to conceal some of the practical problems that crop up in most actual research.

1.   First, theoretical concepts seldom permit unambiguous operationalization.

2. Every empirical indicator has some defects; all could be improved on, and the search for better indicators is an endless one.
3. Second, the empirical associations between variables are almost never perfect.
4. Many variables are related empirically to one another to some extent. Specifying the extent that represents acceptance of the hypothesis and the extent that represents rejection, however, is also an arbitrary act.

G. Ultimately, then, scientists use imperfect indicators of theoretical concepts to discover imperfect associations. And these imperfections conspire with one another against our ability to demonstrate cause and effect.

XX. *The Interchangeability of Indexes*

A. Paul Lazarsfeld (1959), in his discussions of the interchangeability of indexes, has provided an important conceptual tool for our understanding of the relationship between measurement and association. He recognized that there are several possible indicators for any ❂ ❂ ❂ .

1. Using the notion of the interchangeability of indexes, a theoretical hypothesis is accepted as a general proposition if it is confirmed by all the specified empirical tests.

B. The implication of the preceding comments is that measurement and association are ❂ ❂ ❂ .

1. The measurement of a variable makes little sense outside the empirical and theoretical contexts of the associations to be tested.
2. The "proper" way of measuring a given variable depends heavily on the variables to be associated with it.

KEY NAMES AND TERMS

idiographic model of explanation
nomothetic model of explanation
necessary cause
sufficient cause
micromediational
molar
validity

Multiple Choice Questions

1.   The idiographic model of explanation

       a.   uses idioms to explain behavior.
       b.   probes the multiplicity of reasons that account for a specific behavior.
       c.   utilizes only a small number of considerations in reaching an explanation.
       d.   considers only one reason in accounting for a behavior.

2.   A necessary cause would be one that

       a.   has to appear and then disappear in order for the effect to follow.
       b.   has to be absent in order for the effect to follow.
       c.   has to be present in order for the effect to follow.
       d.   guarantees that the effect will follow.

3.   A micromediational causal statement is one that

       a.   gives a detailed explanation about why something happens.
       b.   gives a vague explanation about why something happens.
       c.   mediates a relationship between two variables.
       d.   studies only one small detail which explains why something occurs.

4.   Concern with whether we are correct in inferring that a cause produced some effect is known as

       a.   inferential statistics.
       b.   correlation.
       c.   deconstructed validity.
       d.   validity of causal inference.

5.   Which of the following is a common threat to statistical conclusion validity?

       a.   lack of good measures of dependent or independent variable.
       b.   basing conclusions on a small number of cases.
       c.   when a third variable explains the relationship between the independent and dependent variables (spuriousness).
       d.   both a and b are a common threats to statistical conclusion validity.

6.　　Construct validity refers to

    a.　　generalizing from what we observe and measure to the real-world things in which we are interested.
    b.　　generalizing from the real-world things we observe to see if they are real.
    c.　　ignoring measurement and focusing on how a concept is built.
    d.　　determining whether or not research findings from one study could be reproduced in another study.

7.　　The correspondence between basic research under controlled conditions and the real-world application of research findings refers to

    a.　　construct validity.
    b.　　statistical conclusion validity.
    c.　　external validity.
    d.　　causal inference.

8.　　Which one of the following statements characterizes the deterministic model of human behavior?

    a.　　Not all human actions, feelings, and beliefs are determined.
    b.　　All humans are controlled by the same basic factors.
    c.　　There is no such thing as free will.
    d.　　Causal patterns are simple.

9.　　A scientists argues that drinking contributes to violent behavior. this is an example of

    a.　　molar causal statement.
    b.　　micromediational causal statement.
    c.　　axiom.
    d.　　principle.

10.　　Consider the relationship between the following two variables: committing a criminal act, and being arrested. Committing a criminal act represents which type of cause in this relationship?

    a.　　conditional
    b.　　necessary
    c.　　correlational
    d.　　sufficient

11. A researcher is interested in examining the effect of cocaine use on aggressive behavior. She has recruited 20 volunteers for her study. This researcher should be particularly concerned about threats to which type of validity, due to the small number of subjects?

    a. external validity
    b. construct validity
    c. statistical conclusion validity
    d. internal validity

12. Professor Johnson conducted a carefully controlled laboratory experiment to assess the effect of offender attitudes and demeanor on police decision whether to arrest. He is worried that the results found in his study will not correspond to real-life police encounters. He is concerned about threats to which type of validity?

    a. external validity
    b. construct validity
    c. statistical conclusion validity
    d. internal validity

13. A researcher is interested in evaluating the effectiveness of a drug treatment program. The program started out with 500 patients, and by the end of the treatment period, only 275 patients were still participating. The researcher interviewed these 275 individuals one year after completion of the program and asked about drug use. Since a relatively higher percentage of these subjects remained clean during that year, the researcher concluded that the program is extremely effective. The researcher appears to have overlooked the fact that the most unsuccessful patients dropped out early. Threats to which type of validity are clearly a problem here?

    a. external validity
    b. construct validity
    c. statistical conclusion validity
    d. internal validity

14. Which one of the following is not one of the criteria for causality?

    a. The independent variable must occur earlier in time than the dependent variable.
    b. The observed relationship cannot be explained away as the artificial product of the effect of another, earlier variable.
    c. The independent variable must not be related to any other dependent variables.
    d. The independent and dependent variables must be empirically related to one another.

15. The nomothetic model of explanation

    a.   involves the enumeration of the many possible considerations that underlie a phenomenon.
    b.   has been considered less dehumanizing than the idiographic model of explanation.
    c.   is probabilistic in its approach to causation.
    d.   seeks total explanation of a phenomenon.

16. Consider the relationship between smoking crack and testing positive on a urinalysis for drug use. Smoking crack represents which type of cause in this relationship?

    a.   conditional
    b.   sufficient
    c.   necessary
    d.   necessary and sufficient

17. The interchangeability of indicators involves

    a.   using several possible indicators to represent a variable.
    b.   exchanging one variable for another when results indicate that no empirical relationship exists.
    c.   using several non-related indicators to represent a variable.
    d.   using one indicator at a time to assess which indicator best represents a variable.

18. Consider the relationship between spending time in prison and being released on parole. Spending time in prison represents which type of cause in this relationship?

    a.   conditional
    b.   sufficient
    c.   necessary
    d.   necessary and sufficient

19. A researcher finds that adolescents who drop out of school are more likely to use drugs than their in-school peers. This researcher concludes that dropping out of school causes drug use. Which finding would indicate that this causal explanation may be incorrect?

    a.   The drop-outs did not use drugs while in school.
    b.   Dropping out of school and drug use are statistically correlated.
    c.   Poor self-esteem is related to both drug use and dropping out of school.
    d.   All of the above point to an alternative explanation.

20.   You are interested in examining the effect of understanding the dangers of AIDS on sexual promiscuity. You conduct a study in which a large group of students is randomly assigned to either an experimental or control group. Both groups are surveyed about their sexual activity. Next, the experimental group watches a highly technical, excessively boring video on the ways in which the HIV virus invades the human body. A month later, both groups are surveyed about their sexual activity. Feedback from the experimental subjects indicates that some students actually fell asleep during the video, while others found it very difficult to comprehend. You are concerned that watching the video does not adequately represent an acquired understanding of the dangers of AIDS. This concern relates to threats to which type of validity?

    a.   internal validity
    b.   construct validity
    c.   statistical conclusion validity
    d.   external validity

True/False Questions

1.   Threats to internal validity often have their sources in nonrandom or systematic errors.

    a.   true
    b.   false

2.   The two basic categories of types of validity threats are bias and generalizability.

    a.   true
    b.   false

3.   One of the chief goals of the scientist, social or other, is to explain why things are the way they are.

    a.   true
    b.   false

4.   Social scientists realize that the concept of "free will" is deterministic in nature.

    a.   true
    b.   false

5.   The nomothetic model of explanation differs from the idiographic model in that it does not involve an exhaustive enumeration of all the considerations that result in a particular action or event.

a.   true
b.   false

6.   Unfortunately, social science researchers are limited in that they are not able to make causal statements, since there are always exceptions to any given rule.

a.   true
b.   false

7.   By definition, causes can never be both necessary and sufficient.

a.   true
b.   false

8.   When the average citizen states "the flipping of the switch causes the light to turn on," they are actually making a molar statement.

a.   true
b.   false

9.   Researchers can plan to reduce potential threats to internal validity.

a.   true
b.   false

10. In a general sense, external validity is concerned with whether research findings from one study can be reproduced in another study, often under different conditions.

a.   true
b.   false

Essay Questions

1.   How does determinism relate to criminal justice research? Compare this idea with the idea of free will. What do you believe more closely describes human behavior? Why.

2.   Select a theory of delinquency and briefly describe/outline a way to study if the selected theory does a good job of explaining today's youthful misbehavior. Continue by listing and defining four types of validity threats. Finally, apply the threats to validity (that you have identified) as they could affect the study that you have briefly described.

3. How is the interchangeability of indexes related to understanding the relationship between measurement and association?

Chapter 4

GENERAL ISSUES IN RESEARCH DESIGN

Chapter Outline

I.   *Introduction*

    A.   Research design, the topic of this chapter, addresses the planning of scientific inquiry—designing a strategy for finding out something. There are two major aspects of research design.

         1.   You must specify ◐ ◐ ◐

         2.   You must determine ◐ ◐ ◐

    B.   Ultimately, scientific inquiry comes down to making observations ◐ ◐ ◐

    C.   This chapter provides a general introduction to research design. It is important in Part 2 to realize that in practice, all aspects of research design are interrelated.

II.   *Purposes of Research*

    ◇   Criminal justice research, of course, serves many purposes. Four of the most common and useful purposes are *exploration*, ◐ ◐ ◐

III. *Exploration*

    A.   Much research in criminal justice is conducted to explore the nature or frequency of a problem, or in some cases types of policy.

    B.   An exploratory project might also collect data on some measure to establish a baseline against which ◐ ◐ ◐

    C.   Exploratory studies are also appropriate when some type of policy change is being considered.

    D.   Exploratory research in criminal justice can be simple or complex, using a ◐ ◐ ◐

E. An exploratory study may also be conducted to develop methods that will be used in a more careful study in the future.

IV. *Description*

    A. A major purpose of many criminal justice studies is to describe the scope of crime problems or ❂❂❂ .

        1. Criminal justice observation and description uses methods grounded in social sciences, and strives to be more accurate than casual observations people may make about social issues.

        2. Descriptive studies are often concerned with counting or documenting observations, while exploratory studies focus more on developing a ❂❂❂ .

    B. Because criminal justice policy in the United States is almost exclusively under the control of state and local governments, many descriptive studies seek to obtain and summarize information from local governments.

    C. The **generalizability** of descriptive research is also important. One way to think about the generalizability of description is to consider how well a study of a particular group of subjects represents ❂❂❂ .

V. *Explanation*

    ✧ A third general purpose of criminal justice research is to explain things.

VI. *Application*

    A. Applied research is fundamentally based on a need for specific facts and findings with policy implications. Another purpose for criminal justice research is therefore its application to public policy.

    B. This section will focus on two major types of research for the purpose of application.

        1. Social science research methods are often used to evaluate the effects of specific criminal justice programs. Evaluation involves comparing the goals of a program to its results.

45

2.   The second type of applied research is policy analysis. Rather than observing and analyzing current or past behavior, policy analysis is prospective in trying to anticipate ❂ ❂ ❂   .

VII.   *Units of Analysis*

✧   In criminal justice research there is a great deal of variation in what or who is studied: what are technically called ❂ ❂ ❂   .

1   You then combine the descriptions of many individuals to provide a descriptive picture of the population that comprises those individuals.
2.   Units of analysis in a study are typically also the *units of observation*.
3.   Units of analysis, then, are those units or things we examine in order to create summary descriptions of all such units and ❂ ❂ ❂   .

VIII.   *Individuals*

✧   The norm of *generalized understanding* in social science should suggest that scientific findings are most valuable when they apply to all kinds of people.

1.   At this point, it is enough to realize that descriptive studies having individuals as their units of analysis typically aim to describe the population that comprises those individuals.
2.   As the units of analysis, individuals may be considered in the context of their ❂ ❂ ❂   .

IX.   *Groups*

✧   Social groups may also be the units of analysis for criminal justice research.

✧   Units of analysis at the group level could be households, city blocks, census tracts, cities, counties, or other geographic regions, etc.

X.   *Organizations*

✧   Formal political or social *organizations* may also be units of analysis in criminal justice research.

1.   Examples of formal organizations suitable as units of analysis would be police departments, courtrooms, probation offices, drug treatment facilities, and victim services agencies, etc.

2. When social groups or formal organizations are the units of analysis, their characteristics are often derived from the characteristics of their individual members.

XI. *Social Artifacts*

A. Another large group of possible units of analysis may be referred to generally as social artifacts, or the ❂ ❂ ❂   .

    1. One class of artifacts would be such social objects as fictional accounts of crime depicted in mystery books, television dramas, feature films, or country-western songs.

    2. Each of these objects implies a population of all such objects: all mass media stories about crime, all newspaper stories about crime, all weekly newsmagazine features about crime, all television news reports about crime, all editorial comments about crime, all letters to the editor about crime.

B. Social interactions form another large class of social artifacts suitable for criminal justice research.

    1. Records of different types of social interactions are common units of analysis in criminal justice research.

    2. Police crime reports criminal history records, meetings of community anticrime groups, presentence investigations, and interactions between police and citizens are examples.

XII. *Units of Analysis in Review*

   ◇ The purpose of this section has been to stretch your imagination regarding possible units of analysis for criminal justice research.

    1. Although individual human beings are often the units of analysis, that ❂ ❂ ❂   .

    2. Many research questions can more appropriately be answered through the examination of other units of analysis.

    3. It is essential to ❂ ❂ ❂   .

XIII. *The Ecological Fallacy*

   ◇ The danger of making assertions about individuals as the unit of analysis based on the examination of groups or other aggregations.

1.   Often a criminal justice researcher must address a particular question through an ecological analysis when, for example, the most appropriate data are simply not available.
2.   The danger here lies in drawing unwarranted assumptions about the causes of those patterns—assumptions about individuals making up the group.

IX.   *Reductionism*

    ◇   Refers to an overly strict limitation on the kinds of concepts and variables to be considered as causes in explaining the broad range of human behavior represented by crime and criminal justice policy.

        1.   Reductionism of any type tends to ◐ ◐ ◐

        2.   Like the ecological fallacy, reductionism occurs with the use of inappropriate units of analysis.
        3.   The appropriate unit of analysis for a given research question is not always clear, and it is often debated by social scientists, especially across disciplinary boundaries.

XV.   *The Time Dimension*

    ◇   Time plays a number of different roles in the design and execution of research, aside from the time it takes to do research.

        1.   We described in Chapter 3 how the time sequence of events and situations is ◐ ◐ ◐
        2.   Time is also involved in the generalizability of research findings.
        3.   In general, our observations may be made more or less at one time point, or they may be deliberately ◐ ◐ ◐

XVI.   *Cross-Sectional Studies*

    A.   Many criminal justice research projects are designed to study some phenomenon by taking a cross section of it at one time and analyzing that cross section carefully.

        1.   Exploratory and descriptive studies are often **cross-sectional**.
        2.   A single U.S. Census, for instance is a study aimed at describing ◐ ◐ ◐

B. Cross-sectional studies for explanatory or evaluation purposes have an inherent problem. Typically their aim is to understand causal processes that occur over time, but their conclusions are based on ❂ ❂ ❂ .

XVII. *Longitudinal Studies*

A. Other research projects called **longitudinal studies** are designed to permit ❂ ❂ ❂ .

◇ An example is a researcher who observes the activities of a neighborhood anticrime organization from the time of its inception until its demise.

B. Three special types of longitudinal studies should be noted here:

1. **Trend studies** are those that study ❂ ❂ ❂ .

2. **Cohort studies** examine more specific populations (cohorts) as they change over time.
3. **Panel studies** are similar to trend and cohort studies except that the same set of people is interviewed at two or more time periods. Panel studies are often used in evaluation research, where the same persons are interviewed before and after a new program is introduced.

C. Longitudinal studies have an obvious advantage over cross-sectional ones in providing information about ❂ ❂ ❂ .

1. Often this advantage comes at a heavy cost in both time and money, especially in a large-scale study that follows subjects for many years.
2. Panel studies, which offer the most comprehensive data on changes over time, face a special problem: panel attrition, which ❂ ❂ ❂ .

XVIII. *Approximating Longitudinal Studies*

A. Often it is possible to draw approximate conclusions about processes that take place over time, even when only cross-sectional data are available.

B. Logical inferences may be made whenever the time order of variables is clear. Thus, even though our observations were made at only one time, we might feel justified in drawing conclusions about processes taking place across time.

XIX. *Retrospective Studies*

    A.   Retrospective research, which asks people to recall their pasts, is another common way of approximating observations over time.

        ♦   A study of recidivism, for example, might select a group of persons in prison and analyze their prior history of delinquency or crime.

    B.   The danger of these techniques are evident.

        1.   Sometimes people have ◐◑◐

        2.   Retrospective studies that analyze records of past arrests or convictions suffer different problems. Records may ◐◑◐

        3.   A more fundamental issue in the retrospective approach hinges on how subjects are selected, and how subject selection affects the kinds of research questions that retrospective studies can address.

    C.   Robert Sampson and John Laub (1993:14) comment on how retrospective and prospective views yield different interpretations ◐◑◐

        1.   We do not suggest that retrospective studies are without value. Rather, we want to sensitize you to how the time dimension is linked to a framing of research questions.

        2.   A retrospective approach is limited in its ability to reveal ◐◑◐

XX. *The Time Dimension Summarized*

    A.   The following is a clever metaphor that distinguishes different types of longitudinal studies from cross-sectional ones.

    B.   Think of a cross-sectional study as a snapshot, a trend study as a slide show, and a panel study as ◐◑◐

        1.   A cross-sectional study, like a snapshot, produces an image at one point in time.

        2.   Think of a slide show as a series of snapshots, in sequence over time. By viewing a slide show, we can tell how some indicator varies over time.

        3.   A panel study, like a motion picture, can capture moving images of the same individuals, giving us information about individual observations over time.

C.   In designing any study, you need to look at both ◐◐◐

      .

1.   Are you interested in describing some process that occurs over time?
2.   If you want to describe a process occurring over time, will you be able to make observations at different points in the process, or will you have to approximate such observations—drawing logical inferences from what you can observe now?

XXI.   How to Design a Research Project

A.   Although research design occurs at the beginning of a research project, it involves all the steps of the subsequent project.

B.   Ultimately, the research process needs to be seen as a whole, and you need to grasp it as a whole in order to ◐◐◐   .

XXII.   The Research Process

A.   At the top of the diagram 4.2 are interests, ideas, theories, and new programs, the possible beginning points for a line of research.

1.   Inquiry might have a general interest in finding out why something occurs.
2.   Your inquiry might begin with a specific idea about the way things are.
3.   Finally, the research process might begin with an idea for a new program.

B.   Any or all of these beginnings may suggest the need for empirical research.

1.   The purpose of such research can be to explore an interest, test a specific idea, validate a complex theory, or ◐◐◐   .
2.   Whatever the purpose, a variety of decisions needs to be made, as indicated in the remainder of the diagram.
3.   You should begin to think about units of analysis and the ◐◐◐

      .

XXIII.   Getting Started

A.   You might do a number of different things to begin pursuing your interests.

1.   You would undoubtedly want to read something about the issue and might begin by finding out what research has been done on the issue.
2.   Newspaper stories could also provide some information on your issue.
3.   You may use the internet to find information relevant to your issue.

4. In addition, you would probably want to talk to people who are affected by, or ❂❂❂ .

5. The purpose of these activities is to prepare you to handle the various research design decisions we are about to examine.

6. As you review previous research literature, you should make note of the designs used by other researchers, asking whether the same designs would ❂❂❂ .

B. It's important that you get a clear understanding about the purpose of your study, before designing your study.

1. Usually, your purpose for undertaking research can be expressed in the form of a report.

2. Specifically, you should get clear about the kinds ❂❂❂ .

XXIV. *Conceptualization*

✧ It is necessary to specify what we mean by concepts in order to do research on them.

1. The first thing you'll have to specify is what you mean by the concept(s) being studied.

2. Obviously, you will need to specify what you mean by the term in your research, but this doesn't necessarily mean you have to settle for a single definition.

3. You will, of course, need to specify all the concepts you wish to study.

XXV. *Choice of Research Method*

✧ A variety of methods are available to the criminal justice researcher. Each of those methods has strengths and weaknesses, and certain concepts are more appropriately studied by some methods than by others.

✧ Usually, the best study design is one that ❂❂❂ .

XXVI. *Population and Sampling*

✧ In addition to refining concepts and measurements, decisions must be made about who or what to study.

1.	The *population* for a study is that group (usually of people) about whom we want to be able to draw conclusions.
2.	We are almost never able to study all the members of the population that interests us, however.
3.	In virtually every case, we must ❍❍❍ .

XXVII.	*Observations*

◇	Having decided what to study among whom by what method, we are now ready to make observations—to ❍❍❍ .

XXVIII.	*Data Processing*

◇	Depending on the research method chosen, you will have amassed a volume of observations in a form that probably isn't easily interpretable. You will need to "make sense" of the observations gathered by organizing all of the collected data.

XXIX.	*Analysis*

◇	Finally, we manipulate the collected data for the purpose of drawing conclusions that reflect on the ❍❍❍ .

XXX.	*Application*

A.	The final stage of the research process involves the uses made of the research you've conducted and the conclusions you've reached.

1.	To start, you will likely want to communicate your findings, so that others will know what you've learned.
2.	Your study might also be useful to actually do something about a specific social problem.

B.	Finally, you should consider what your research ❍❍❍ .

53

XXXI. Review

A. As this overview shows, research design involves a set of decisions regarding what topic is to be studied among *what population* with *what research methods* for *what purpose*.

⬦ Research design is the process of narrowing, of focusing, your perspective for purposes of a particular study.

B. In designing a research project, you will find it useful to begin by assessing three things: your own interests, ◐ ◐ ◐

1. Once you have a few questions you would be interested in answering for yourself, think about the kind of information needed to answer them.
2. What research units of analysis would ◐ ◐ ◐
   ?
3. Then ask which aspects of the units of analysis would provide the information you need to answer your research question.
4. Once you have some ideas about the kind of information relevant to your purpose, ask yourself how you might go about getting that information.
5. If you think you would have to collect your data how would you go about doing that?
6. Keep in mind, however, your own research abilities, the resources available to you, and the time required to complete your research project.
7. Once you have a general idea of what you want to study and how, carefully review previous research in journals, books, and government reports to see how other researchers have addressed the topic and what they have learned about it.

XXXII. Elements of a Research Proposal

A. What exactly do you want to study? Why is it worth studying?

B. What have others said about this topic?

1. What theories address it, and what do they say?
2. What research has ◐ ◐ ◐   ?
3. Are there consistent findings, or do past studies disagree?
4. Are there flaws in the body of existing research that you feel you can remedy?

C. Who or what will you study in order to collect data?

    1. Identify the subjects in general terms, and specifically identify who (or what) is available for study and how you will reach them.
    2. Will it be appropriate to ❂❂❂   ?
    3. If so, how will you do that?

D. What are the key variables in your study?

    1. How will you define and ❂❂❂   ?
    2. Do your definitions and measurement methods duplicate or differ from those of previous research on this topic?

E. How will you actually collect the data for your study?

    1. Will you observe behavior directly or conduct a survey?
    2. Will you undertake field research, or are you going to focus on the reanalysis of data already collected by others?

F. Give some indication of the kind of analysis you plan to conduct.

    ◇   Spell out the purpose and ❂❂❂   of your analysis.

G. It is often appropriate to provide a schedule for the various stages of research.

H. If you are asking someone to give you money to pay the costs of your research, you will need to provide a budget, specifying where the money will go.

    ◇   If you are going to invest your time and energy in such a project, you should do what you can to ensure a return on that investment

KEY NAMES AND TERMS

units of analysis
evaluation
policy analysis
units of observation
generalized understanding
organizations
social artifacts
ecological fallacy
reductionism

individualistic fallacy
cross-sectional
trend studies
cohort studies
panel studies
content analysis
field research
population
triangulation

Multiple Choice Questions

1. Research which is conducted in order to find out the nature of frequency of a problem is

   a. descriptive
   b. exploratory
   c. explanatory
   d. applied

2. Police officers, victims of violent crime and gang members are all examples of which type of units of analysis?

   a. individual
   b. group
   c. organization
   d. social artifacts

3. Ethical considerations regarding research are important because

   a. a research subject may be harmed through embarrassment or violation of privacy.
   b. a research subject may be physically harmed after being seen talking to a researcher.
   c. a research subject may suffer psychological harm from discussing a past trauma, such as being a victim of crime or sexual abuse.
   d. all of the above are important ethical considerations in research.

4. A local police department collects data on the number of armed robberies that have taken place in different city neighborhoods over the past year. The purpose of such research appears to be

   a. explanation
   b. reductionism
   c. description
   d. longitudinal

5.   Determining the effectiveness of a program to reduce drug use is a topic suitable for which of the following purposes of research?

     a.   exploration
     b.   description
     c.   reductionism
     d.   application

6.   A researcher discovers that murder rates are higher in states with high unemployment rates. he concludes that unemployed people are actually committing more murders than employed people. This researcher has made the error of

     a.   drawing conclusions about individuals based solely on the observation of groups.
     b.   limiting the kinds of concepts and variables to be considered as causes.
     c.   making an explanation based solely on environmental factors.
     d.   drawing conclusions about groups or aggregates based solely on the observation of individuals.

7.   A researcher interested in recidivism rates interviews individuals who are released from prison during 1993 and follows up with additional interviews of the same people in 1994 and 1995. This best exemplifies which type of study?

     a.   retrospective
     b.   cross-sectional
     c.   panel
     d.   cohort

8.   Studies based on observations representing one point in time are considered

     a.   explanatory
     b.   longitudinal
     c.   cross-sectional
     d.   fundamental

9.   A government task force plans to examine levels of violence in several Saturday morning cartoons over a three month period. the units of analysis for this research are

     a.   social artifacts
     b.   individuals
     c.   months
     d.   violent acts

10. A criminology graduate student's dissertation examines the question of whether college students who watch more violence on television are more likely to become involved in fights than those who watch less violence. the units of analysis for this research are

   a. groups
   b. individuals
   c. fights
   d. social artifacts

11. Another student's dissertation focuses on the characteristics of drug treatment centers that are related to client success. The units of analysis for this study are

   a. groups
   b. individuals
   c. organizations
   d. social artifacts

12. The main purpose of an institutional review board is to

   a. allocate funds for research projects
   b. review research proposals in an effort to minimize the possibility of copyright infringement.
   c. review research proposals in an effort to minimize the potential harm to subjects.
   d. make decisions regarding units of analysis

13. In the research process described in the text, operationalization refers to

   a. specifying the meaning of concepts and variables to be studied.
   b. the use of research findings in real-life applications.
   c. transforming the data collected into a form appropriate for manipulation and analysis.
   d. specifying the concrete steps that will be used to measure specific concepts.

14. Conceptualization refers to

   a. the development of a theory using well-defined concepts.
   b. specifying the meaning of concepts and variables to be studied.
   c. outlining specific hypotheses to be tested in the research.
   d. specifying the concrete steps that will be used to measure particular concepts.

15. While each funding agency (or instructor) may require specific elements to appear in a research proposal, Maxfield and Babbie outline several of the most common elements. Which of the following is commonly included in a proposal?

    a. analysis
    b. budget
    c. measurement
    d. all of the above

True/False Questions

1. The norm of "generalized understanding" in social science suggests that scientific findings are not valuable if they apply to all kinds of people.

    a. true
    b. false

2. Panel studies consist of interviewing the same specific individuals over a period of time.

    a. true
    b. false

3. A budget should never be considered when designing a research project.

    a. true
    b. false

4. Research in criminal justice is conducted to explore the nature and frequency of a problem, but not for the effectiveness of policy.

    a. true
    b. false

5. An exploratory project might collect data on some measure to establish a baseline against which future changes will be compared.

    a. true
    b. false

6. A third general purpose of criminal justice research is to explain things.

    a. true
    b. false

7. Units of analysis describe the what or who is being studied within a particular piece of research.

    a. true
    b. false

8. Because groups are made up of aggregates, they cannot be used as a unit of analysis for research in criminal justice.

    a. true
    b. false

9. Reductionism refers to poor conclusions based on large samples used in a particular piece of research.

    a. true
    b. false

10. Few exploratory or descriptive studies are considered "cross-sectional."

    a. true
    b. false

Essay Questions

1. What are the elements of a research proposal? Describe and illustrate each step in the process.

2. You're interested in the topic of shock incarceration, also known as boot camps. Briefly outline possible exploratory, descriptive and explanatory research on this topic. Finally, after providing the requested outlines, briefly describe one possible threat to validity for each approach.

Chapter 5

CONCEPTS, OPERATIONALIZATION, AND MEASUREMENT

Chapter Outline

I.   *Introduction*

   A.   This chapter deals with the process of moving from vague ideas about what you want to study to being able to recognize it and measure it in the real world.

   B.   Ultimately, criminal justice and social scientific research seek to communicate findings to an audience--your professor, classmates, readers of a journal, or co-workers in a probation services agency, for example.

      1.   Earlier steps move from vague or general ideas to more precise definitions of critical terms.
      2.   With more precise definitions, we can begin to develop measures that can ◐ ◐ ◐   .

II.   *Conceptions and Concepts*

   A.   Ultimately, concepts are used in communication: a name we use to represent a collection of related phenomena that we have either observed or heard about somewhere.

      1.   For example the word *crime* represents conceptions about certain kinds of behavior. Individual people may have different conceptions; they may think of different kinds of behavior when they hear the word crime.
      2.   Because they are subjective and cannot be communicated directly, we use the words, symbols, and phrases of language as a way of communicating about our conceptions and the things we observe that are related to those conceptions.
      3.   *Concepts* are the words or symbols in language that are used to represent these mental images. We use concepts to communicate with each other, to share our mental images.
      4.   The concept represents things like physical harm to a victim, offender motivation, offender age, weapon use, and what types of punishment might be provided for committing robbery.

   B.   In order to link conceptions, concepts, and measurement, consider Abraham Kaplan's (1964) discussion of three classes of things that scientists measure: direct observables, ◐ ◐ ◐   ,   .

1. Direct observables, includes those things that we can observe simply and directly, like ❂❂❂

2. Indirect observables require "relatively more subtle, complex, or indirect observations" (Kaplan, 1964:55).
3. *Constructs* are theoretical creations ❂❂❂

III. *Conceptualization*

A. Day-to-day communication usually occurs through a system of general but often vague agreements about the use of terms.

1. A wide range of misunderstandings is the price we pay for our imprecision, but somehow we muddle through.
2. Science, however, aims at more than muddling, and it cannot operate in a context of such imprecision.

B. **Conceptualization** is the process through which we specify precisely what we will mean when ❂❂❂

1. These terms are working agreements in the sense that they allow us to work on the question.
2. The end product of this conceptualization process is the specification of a set of indicators of what we have in mind, indicating the presence or absence of the concept we are studying.

C. A **dimension** refers to some ❂❂❂

1. Thus we might speak of the "victim harm dimension" of crime seriousness.
2. This dimension could include indicators of physical injury, economic loss, or psychological consequences.
3. Specifying dimensions and identifying the various indicators for each of those dimensions are both parts of conceptualization.
4. Specifying the different dimensions of a concept often paves the way for a ❂❂❂

IV. *Confusion Over Definitions and Reality*

A Reviewing briefly, our concepts are derived from the mental images (conceptions) that summarize collections of seemingly related experiences.

1. Although the observations and experiences are real, our ❂❂❂

2.	The terms associated with concepts are merely devices created for ❂❂❂

3.	Once we have assumed that terms have real meanings, we begin the tortured task of discovering what those real meanings are and what constitutes a genuine measurement of them.

B.	The process of regarding as real things that are not is called **reification**, and the reification of concepts in day-to-day life is very common.

V.	*Creating Conceptual Order*

A.	Logicians and scientists have found it useful to distinguish three kinds of definitions: real, ❂❂❂ , .

1.	The specification of concepts in scientific inquiry depends on conceptual and operational definitions.
2.	A **conceptual definition** is a ❂❂❂

B.	The specification of conceptual definitions does two important things.

1.	First, it serves as a specific working definition a researcher presents so that readers will ❂❂❂
2.	Second, a conceptual definition helps focus our observational strategy.

C.	The **operational definition** of the concept is a definition that spells out precisely how the concept will be measured. Strictly speaking, an operational definition is a description of the "operations" that will be undertaken in measuring a concept.

D.	**Operationalization** is the process of ❂❂❂

1.	Although you begin by conceptualizing what it is you wish to study, once you start to consider operationalization, you ❂❂❂

2.	Developing an operational definition also moves you closer to measurement which requires that you think, too, about selecting a data-collection method.

VI.	*Measurement*

A.	Operationalization involves describing ❂❂❂

1.	The next step is, of course, making the measurement.

2. Measurement is "the process of assigning numbers or labels to units of analysis in order to represent conceptual properties. This process should be quite familiar to the reader even if the definition is not."

3. Another way to think of measurement is to think of ❂ ❂ ❂

B. Measurement is distinct from operationalization in that measurement involves actually making observation in the real world and assigning scores--numbers or other labels--to those observations.

1. Many people consider measurement the most important, and difficult, stage in conducting criminal justice research. It is difficult, in part, because so many basic concepts in criminal justice are not easy to define as specifically as we would like.

2. Even when we can specify unambiguous conceptual definitions, it is often difficult to specify operational definitions that will enable us to make observations and measurements.

VII. *Exhaustive and Exclusive Measurement*

A. An attribute, you'll recall from Chapter 1, is ❂ ❂ ❂

B. Variables, on the other hand, are logical ❂ ❂ ❂

C. The conceptualization and operationalization processes can be seen as the specification of variables and the attributes composing them.

D. Every variable should have two important qualities.

1. First, the attributes composing it should be *exhaustive*. If the variable is to have any utility in research, you should be able to classify every observation in terms of one of the attributes composing the variable.

2. At the same time, attributes composing a variable must be *mutually exclusive*. You must be able ❂ ❂ ❂

VIII. *Levels of Measurement*

A. Attributes composing any variable must be mutually exclusive and exhaustive. However, attributes may be related in other ways as well.

B. **Nominal Measures** Variables whose attributes have only the characteristics of exhaustiveness and mutual exclusiveness are **nominal measures**.

◇ Nominal measures merely offer names or labels for characteristics.

C. **Ordinal Measures** Variables whose attributes may be logically *rank-ordered* are **ordinal measures.**

    1.   The different attributes represent relatively more or less of the variable.

    2.   Such variables can be ordered in some way, although the actual distance between these orderings ❂ ❂ ❂

D. The logical distance between attributes can be expressed in meaningful standard intervals, when a variable is measured at the **interval level.**

E. In **ratio measures**, the attributes composing a variable besides having all the structural characteristics mentioned previously, ❂ ❂ ❂

VIX.   *Implications of Levels of Measurement*

A. To review this discussion and to understand why level of measurement may make a difference, consider Table 5-1.

B. Specific analytic techniques require variables that meet certain minimum levels of measurement.

C. At the same time, you should realize that some variables may be treated as ❂ ❂ ❂

    1.   Ratio measures are the highest level, descending through interval and ordinal to nominal, the lowest level of measurement.

    2.   A variable representing a given level of measurement--say, ratio--may also be treated as representing a lower level of measurement--say, ordinal.

D. The analytic uses planned for a given variable, then, should determine the level of measurement to be sought, with the realization that some variables are inherently limited to a certain level.

    1.   If a variable is to be used in a variety of ways, requiring different levels of measurement, the study should ❂ ❂ ❂

    2.   But you do not necessarily have to measure variables at their highest level of measurement.

    3.   Whenever your research purposes are not altogether clear, however, it is advisable to seek the highest level of measurement possible.

    4.   More generally, you cannot ❂ ❂ ❂
                . That is a one-way street worth remembering.

X. *Criteria for Measurement Quality*

    A.   Measurements can be made with varying degrees of *precision,* representing the fineness of distinctions made between attributes composing a variable.

        1.   As a general rule, precise measurements are superior to imprecise ones, as common sense would dictate.

        2.   Precision and accuracy are obviously important qualities in research measurement and they probably need no further explanation.

XI.   *Reliability*

    A.   **Reliability** is a matter of whether a particular measurement technique, applied repeatedly to the same object, would yield the same result each time. In other words, measurement reliability is ◑ ◑ ◑

        1.   Reliability, however, does not ◑ ◑ ◑

        2.   Measurement reliability is often a problem with indicators that are commonly used in criminal justice research.

        3.   Other examples of reliability problems may be found in criminal justice research and policy settings.

    B.   Reliability is a concern every time a single observer is the source of data, since we have no way to guard against the impact of that observer is the source of data, since we have no way to guard against the impact of that observer's subjectivity.

        1.   We can't tell for sure how much of what's reported originated in the situation observed and how much in the observer.

        2.   The opposite situation, where more than one observer makes measurements, can also produce reliability problems.

        3.   Similar problems arise whenever we ask people ◑ ◑ ◑

    C.   Because the problem of reliability is a basic one in criminal justice measurement, researchers have developed a number of techniques for dealing with it.

    D.   **Test-Retest Method** Sometimes it is appropriate to make the same measurement ◑ ◑ ◑ .

        1.   If there is no reason to expect the information sought to change, you should expect the same response both times.

        2.   If answers vary, however, that may indicate the measurement method is, to the extent of that variation, unreliable.

3. Although this method can be a useful reliability check, it is limited in some respects. One is illustrated by the West and Farrington study: faulty memory may produce inconsistent responses if there is a long time period between the initial interview and the retest.

4. A different problem can arise in trying to use the test-retest method to check the reliability of attitude or opinion measures. That is if the list retest interval is short, answers given in the second interview may be ◐ ◐ ◐

(i.e., testing bias).

E. **Interrater reliability** It is also possible for measurement unreliability to be generated by research workers--for examples, interviewers and coders.

1. To guard against interviewer unreliability, it is common practice in surveys to have a supervisor call a subsample of the respondents on the telephone and ◐ ◐ ◐   .

2. Comparing measurements from different raters works in other situations as well.

3. One way to increase the consistency of translating official records for example, a process often referred to as *coding*, is to have more than one person code a sample of records, and compare the consistency of coding decisions made by each person.

F. As a general rule, it is always a good idea to make more than one measurement of any subtle or complex social concept, such as prejudice or fear of crime.

◇ If the two sets of items measure people differently, that, again, ◐ ◐ ◐
                                                    .

G. The reliability of measurements is a fundamental issue in criminal justice research, however, we hasten to point out that even total reliability doesn't ensure that our measures ◐ ◐ ◐   .

XII. *Validity*

A. In conventional usage, the term **validity** refers to the extent to which an empirical measure ◐ ◐ ◐   .

1. Put another way, measurement validity means ◐ ◐ ◐
                                                    ?

2. Recall that an operational definition specifies the operations you will perform to measure a concept. Does your operational definition accurately reflect the concept you are interested in?

3. While methods for assessing reliability are relatively straightforward, it is more difficult to demonstrate that individual measures are valid.

4. Researchers have some ways of dealing with the issue of validity.

B. First, there's something called **face validity**. Particular empirical measures may or may not be with our common agreements and our individual mental images associated with a particular concept.

> ✧ There are many concrete agreements among researchers about how to measure certain basic concepts.

C. **Content validity** refers to the ❂ ❂ ❂   .

D. **Criterion-related validity** compares a measures to ❂ ❂ ❂   .

1. A measure can be validated by showing that it predicts scores on another measure that is generally accepted as valid; this is something referred to as ❂ ❂ ❂   .

2. Another approach to criterion-related validity is to show that your measure of a concept is different from measures of similar but distinct concepts. This is called *discriminant validity*, meaning that ❂ ❂ ❂   .

3. Sometimes it is difficult to find behavioral criteria that can be taken to validate measures as directly as in the examples above. In those instances, however, we can often approximate such criteria by considering how the variable in question ought, theoretically, to relate to other variables.

E. **Construct validity** is based on the logical relationships among ❂ ❂ ❂   .

1. In addition to developing your measure, you will have also developed certain theoretical expectations about the way the variable ❂ ❂ ❂   .

2. If your measure relates to other variables in the expected fashion, that constitutes evidence of your measure's construct validity.

3. Tests of construct validity, then, can offer a weight of evidence that your measure either does or doesn't tap the quality you want it to measure, without providing definitive proof.

F. Another approach to validation of an individual measure is to compare it to alternative measures of ❂ ❂ ❂   .

> ✧ If someone admits having been arrested for robbery, for example, they could be asked when and where the arrest occurred. Self-reports can then be validated by checking police arrest records.

XIII.   *Composite Measures*

    A.   Sometimes it is possible to construct a single measure that captures the variable of interest. But other variables may be better measured ◐ ◐ ◐

         ✧   For example, the FBI crime index is a composite measure of crime that combines police reports for seven different offenses into one indicator.

    B.   Composite measures are frequently used in criminal justice research for several reasons.

         1.   First, despite the care taken in designing studies to provide valid and reliable measurements of variables, the researcher is often unable to develop in advance single indicators of complex concepts.

         2.   Second, you may wish to employ a rather refined ordinal measure of a variable, arranging cases in several ordinal categories from--for example-- very low to very high on a variable such as degree of parental supervision.

         3.   Finally, indexes and scales are *efficient* devices for data analysis. If considering a single data item gives us only a rough indication of a given variable, considering several data items may give us a more comprehensive and more accurate indication. Composite measures are efficient data-reduction devices.

XIV.   *Typologies*

    A.   Researchers combine variables in different ways to produce different types of composite measures. The simplest of these is a *typology*, sometimes termed a ◐ ◐ ◐

         ✧   Typologies are produced by the intersection of two or more variables, thereby ◐ ◐ ◐

XV.   *An Index of Disorder*

    A.   "What is disorder, and what isn't?" asks Wesley Skogan (1990:4), in his book on the links between crime, fear, and social problems such as public drinking, drug use, litter, prostitution, panhandlers, dilapidated buildings, and groups of boisterous youth.

         1.   In an influential article, 'Broken Windows," James Wilson and George Kelling (1982) described disorder as signs of crime that may contribute independently to fear and crime itself: But how would you measure it?

2. First, we could focus on the *physical presence* of disorder--whether litter, public drinking, public drug use and the like were actually evident in an urban neighborhood.

3. We might measure the physical presence of disorder through a series of systematic observation.

4. The second conception focuses on the *perception* of disorder, recognizing that some people might view, for example, public drinking as disorderly while others (New Orleans residents) considered public drinking to be perfectly acceptable.

5. In order to represent the concept of disorder more completely, we should measure additional behaviors or characteristics that represent other examples of disorder.

6. Skogan created two indexes, one of social disorder and one for physical disorder, by adding up the scores for each item and dividing by the number or items in each group.

B. This example illustrates how several related variables can be combined to produce an index that has certain desirable properties.

1. First, a composite index is a ❍ ❍ ❍

2. Second, computing and average across all items in a category creates more variation in the index than we could obtain in any single item.

3. Finally, two indexes are more parsimonious than nine individual variables; data analysis and interpretation can be ❍ ❍ ❍   .

XVI. *Measurement Summary*

A. We have covered substantial ground in this chapter, but still only introduced the important and often complex issue of measurement in criminal justice research.

◇ Measurement involves continual thinking about the conceptual properties you wish to study, how you will operationalize those properties, and how you will ❍ ❍ ❍   .

KEY NAMES AND TERMS

concepts	ordinal measures
conceptualization	precision
reification	convergent validity
conceptual definition	discriminant validity
exhaustive	typology
mutually exclusive	nominal measures

Multiple Choice Questions

1. Which of the following are one of the three classes of things that scientists measure?

    a. direct observables.
    b. non-observables.
    c. serious crimes.
    d. dimensions

2. An indicator of the dimension "victim harm" is

    a. economic gain.
    b. job opportunity.
    c. physical injury.
    d. police involvement.

3. Being able to rank-order the attributes of a variable indicates which level of measurement?

    a. nominal.
    b. ordinal.
    c. interval.
    d. ratio.

4. When a supervisor for a survey telephones a subset of the respondents to verify certain information, it is an example of

    a. mistrust of the survey workers.
    b. a telephone backup procedure.
    c. inter-rater reliability.
    d. the split-half method.

5. Which of the following is a source of measurement error for the FBI's Uniform Crime Reports?

    a. it does not count all crimes reported to police.
    b. individual states have varying definitions of certain crimes.
    c   if multiple crimes are committed, only the most serious one gets reported in the UCR.
    d. all of the above are potential source(s) of measurement error in measuring crime.

6.   Dr. Czora is interested in attempting to verify information regarding a crime survey which she has conducted. He finds police records of crimes and interviews victims to see if respondents recall being victimized. This method is known as

    a.   the split-half method.
    b.   a forward records check.
    c.   a reverse records check.
    d.   a summary based measure.

7.   Which one of the following if not a technique used to assess the reliability of a measure?

    a.   split-half method
    b.   interrater reliability
    c.   test-retest method
    d.   intersubject reliability

8.   Annual salary (in dollars) would be an example of which level of measurement?

    a.   ratio
    b.   interval
    c.   nominal
    d.   ordinal

9.   Frequency of alcohol use measured in terms of [never, once a month or less, 2-5 times per month, or 6 or more times per month] would be an example of which level of measurement?

    a.   ratio
    b.   interval
    c.   nominal
    d.   ordinal

10.   The number of offenses committed by a subject would be an example of which level of measurement?

    a.   ratio
    b.   interval
    c.   nominal
    d.   ordinal

11. The split-half method of assessing the reliability of a measure involves

    a.   randomly splitting orders into two groups and comparing the results.
    b.   making the same measurement on two separate occasions and comparing the results.
    c.   comparing two randomly selected sets of indicators from a questionnaire.
    d.   randomly splitting the subjects into two groups and comparing the responses.

12. Criterion-related validity refers to

    a.   the degree to which a measure covers the range of meanings included within the concept.
    b.   the degree to which a measure relates to other variables as expected within a system of theoretical relationships.
    c.   the degree to which a measure relates to some external measure of the same concept, generally accepted as valid.
    d.   the degree to which a measure meets the generally accepted criteria for validity.

13. The use of multiple measures to validate an individual measure involves

    a.   taking repeated measures of some concept over an extended period of time.
    b.   comparing a measure to alternative, though not necessarily more accurate measures of the same concept.
    c.   comparing a measure to alternative measures of the same concept, generally accepted as valid.
    d.   replication by individuals coders, with subsequent examination of the agreement among them.

14. Which one of the following sources of measurement error is **not** characteristic of the Uniform Crime Reports (UCR)?

    a.   the operational definition of crime can vary from state to state
    b.   the hierarchy rule is used by police agencies and the FBI to classify crimes
    c.   the UCR includes Part I crimes, only if a person has been arrested and charged with a crime.
    d.   individual states, cities, and counties vary in the quality and completeness of crime data.

15. Which of the following crimes could not be systematically counted by interviewing household members as a part of a victimization survey? (you may choose more than one)

    a.   assault
    b.   public intoxication
    c.   shoplifting
    d.   auto theft

True/False Questions

1.   Precision is the same as accuracy in criminal justice research.

    a.   true
    b.   false

2.   Operationalization involves describing how actual measurements will be made.

    a.   true
    b.   false

3.   Ultimately, criminal justice and social scientific research seek to communicate findings to some audience.

    a.   true
    b.   false

4.   The word crime represents conceptions about behavior. The word crime also represents a concept that researchers understand and agree upon its meaning.

    a.   true
    b.   false

5.   According to Kaplan's (1964) scheme, the concept "anger" exemplifies something he referred to as a direct observable.

    a.   true
    b.   false

6.   Conceptualization is the process through which we specify precisely what we will mean when we use particular terms.

    a.   true
    b.   false

7.   A dimension refers to some specifiable aspect of a direct observable.

    a.   true
    b.   false

8.   Nominal levels of measurement are known to be the most sophisticated of all measures.

    a.   true
    b.   false

9.   Variables can be considered to be logical sets of attributes.

        a.   true
        b.   false

10.   The test-retest method is used to examine a measurements validity.

        a.   true
        b.   false

Essay Questions

1.   Explain how a measure can be reliable but not valid. Which is more important? Do you
        believe that the Federal Bureau of Investigations annual publication the "Uniform Crime
        Report" can be described as being a reliable but not valid measure of crime in America?

2.   Describe a theory of delinquency and outline its major assumptions. Continue by
        identifying and briefly discussing two concepts used in the development of the selected
        theory. Finally, operationalize the identified concepts and consider the issues of reliability
        and validity of the concepts that have been operationalized.

Chapter 6

MEASURING CRIME

Chapter Outline

I.   *Introduction*

    A.   Having discussed the principles of measurement and measurement quality at some length, our attention now turns to a basic measurement task for criminal justice researchers: ❂ ❂ ❂

        1.   Crime is a fundamental dependent variable for criminal justice and criminology.

        2.   *Explanatory studies* frequently seek to learn what causes crime, while applied studies often focus on ❂ ❂ ❂

        3.   *Descriptive and exploratory studies* may simply wish to count how much crime there is in ❂ ❂ ❂

    B.   Crime can also be an independent variable, as in a study of how crime affects fear or other attitudes, or in determining whether people who live in high crime areas are more likely to support long prison sentences for drug dealers.

        1.   Sometimes crime can be both an independent and dependent variable, as in trying to learn about the relationships between drug use and other offenses.

        2.   Whatever your research purpose, and regardless of whether you're interested in what causes crime or what crime causes, it should be clear that measuring crime is important.

II.   *General Issues in Measuring Crime*

    ◇   At the outset, you should be aware of some broad considerations that ❂ ❂ ❂

        1.   The first thing you should think about is what offenses you want to measure.

        2.   We'll discuss different units of analysis implicit in different measures and remind you about the question of ❂ ❂ ❂

III.   *What Offenses?*

    ✧   Let's begin by agreeing on a conceptual definition of crime, one that will enable us to decide ❂❂❂   .

        1.   The authors highlight one of the principal difficulties encountered in trying to measure crime: many different types of behaviors and actions are included in our conceptualization of crime as an: "...act committed in violation of a law that prohibits it and authorizes punishment for its commission."

        2.   Different measures tend to focus on different types of crime, primarily because not all crimes can be measured the same way with any degree of reliability or validity.

IV.   *What Units of Analysis?*

    A.   Recall that units of analysis are the specific entities researchers collect information about.

    B.   Crimes involve four elements that are often easier to recognize in the abstract than they are to actually measure.

        1.   The offender is one possible ❂❂❂   .
        2.   Crimes also require some sort of victim, the second possible unit of analysis.
        3.   For now you should recognize that surveying individuals, organizations, and society involve fundamentally different tasks.
        4.   The final two units of analysis are closely intertwined, and will be discussed together: *offense*, and ❂❂❂   .

V.   *What Purpose?*

    ✧   Different strategies for measuring crime can also be distinguished by their general purpose. Approaches to measuring crime have at least one of three general purposes:

        1.   monitoring
        2.   ❂❂❂
        3.   research

VI.   *Crimes Known to Police*

♦   It's safe to say that the most widely used measures of crime are based on police records, and commonly referred to as ⊕ ⊕ ⊕   .

1.   We emphasize this phrase because it has important implications for understanding what police records ⊕ ⊕ ⊕   .

2.   Certain types of crimes are detected almost exclusively by *observation*—traffic offenses and so-called "victimless" crimes.

3.   Most other crimes, however, are detected and counted because they are *reported to police by other people*: victims or witnesses.

4.   If you recognize that police measure crime in these two ways—crimes they observe or discover themselves, and crimes reported to them—you should be able to think of crimes that are not well measured by police records.

5.   The other way police measure crime is also imperfect. Many crimes are not reported to police, especially minor thefts and certain types of assaults.

6.   Another problem with police measurement of crime undermines the meaning of the commonly used phrase "crimes known to police." Research has shown what some people may have personally experienced: police do not always make official records of crimes they observe or crimes reported to them.

VII.   *Uniform Crime Reports*

A.   Police measures of crime form the basis for the FBI's Uniform Crime Reports, a data series that has been collected since 1930 and has been widely used by criminal justice researchers.

♦   Because UCR data are based on crimes reported to police, they share the measurement problems mentioned above.

B.   However, the FBI crime counts include three additional sources of measurement error.

1.   First, the UCR does not ⊕ ⊕ ⊕   .

2.   Second, one of the reasons Part II offenses are counted only if an arrest is made is that individual states may have varying definitions of these crimes.

3.   Another problem is that individual states, cities, and counties vary in the quality and completeness of crime data sent to the FBI and reported in the annual UCR publication, *Crime in the United States*.

4.   UCR data can also suffer from a variety of clerical, ⊕ ⊕ ⊕

5.   The third source of measurement error in the UCR is produced by the *hierarchy rule* used by police agencies and the FBI to classify crimes. The hierarchy rule means simply that ❂ ❂ ❂

VIII.   *UCR and Criteria for Measurement Quality*

A.   Let's now consider how using the UCR to operationalize and measure crime satisfies the criteria for measurement quality.

    1.   You should readily see that the UCR is neither ❂ ❂ ❂

    2.   Since the UCR does not count all crimes, we can rightly question its ❂ ❂ ❂

    3.   Finally, is the UCR a reliable measure? Not all law enforcement agencies submit complete reports to the FBI, and the quality of the data submitted varies.

B.   Before moving on to other approaches to measuring crime, consider how units of analysis figure into UCR data.

    1.   The UCR system produces what is referred to as a summary-based measure of crime.

    2.   UCR data therefore represent groups as units of analysis.

    3.   Recall that it is possible to aggregate units of analysis to higher levels, but it is not possible to disaggregate grouped data to the individual level.

    4.   Analysis of UCR data is therefore restricted to analysis of such groupings as cities, counties, states, or regions.

IX.   *Incident-Based Police Records*

◇   The U.S. Department of Justice sponsors two series of crime measures that are based on *incidents* as units of analysis.

    1.   The first of these, ❂ ❂ ❂   (SHR)

    2.   Local law enforcement agencies submit detailed information about individual homicide incidents under the SHR program.

    3.   Because it is an incident-based system, measuring homicides with SHR data make it possible to conduct a variety of descriptive and explanatory studies that examine individual events. (Notice that such analyses would not be possible if we were studying homicide using UCR summary data.)

4. Crime measures based on incidents as units of analysis therefore have several advantages over summary measures. However, remember that SHR data still ❂ ❂ ❂

X. *National Incident-Based Reporting System*

A. The most recent development in police-based measures at the national level is the ongoing effort by the FBI and the Bureau of Justice Statistics (BJS) to convert the UCR to a National Incident-Based Reporting System (NIBRS).

1. The main difference between NIBRS and the UCR system—reporting each crime incident rather than the total number of certain crimes for each law enforcement agency.
2. Referring back to our earlier discussion of incidents, offenders, offenses, and victims, you should realize that information found in NIBRS is ❂ ❂ ❂

3. Collecting detailed information on each incident for each offense, victim, and offender, and doing so for a large number of offense types, represent the most significant changes in NIBRS compared to the UCR.

B. NIBRS incorporates a number of other revisions, summarized from a publication on NIBRS guidelines (FBI, 1988:12-20):

1. Victim Type
2. ❂ ❂ ❂
3. Computer-base submission
4. ❂ ❂ ❂
5. Computers and crime
6. Quality control

XI. *NIBRS and Criteria for Measurement Quality*

◇ How does incident-based reporting fare on our criteria for measurement quality?

1. Eliminating the hierarchy rule means offense classifications are mutually exclusive. Is NIBRS exhaustive? Because Group B offenses are recorded only for crimes that result in arrest, not all crimes are counted.
2. In at least one sense, NIBRS data hold the promise of ❂ ❂ ❂
The FBI has produced very thorough documentation on how to record and classify incidents and their component records.
3. Creating auditing standards and requiring submission of data on computer-readable media also enhances reliability.

4.   Finally, the FBI requires that state records systems be certified before they can submit incident-based reports.

XII.   *Measuring Crime Through Surveys*

A.   Conducting a survey that asks people whether or not they have been the victim of a crime is one alternative measure of crime.

B.   In principle, measuring crime through a survey has several advantages.

1.   Surveys can obtain information on crimes that ❂ ❂ ❂
2.   Asking people about victimizations can also measure incidents that police may not have officially recorded as crimes.
3.   If conducted in a rigorous, systematic fashion, surveys ❂ ❂ ❂

4.   Finally, asking individual people about crimes that may have happened to them provides data on victims and offenders (individuals), and the incidents themselves (social artifacts).

XIII.   *National Crime Victimization Survey*

A.   Since 1972, the U.S. Census Bureau has conducted the ❂ ❂ ❂
                                                for these and other reasons.

1.   One of the primary reasons for conducting crime surveys was to illuminate what came to be referred to as the "❂ ❂ ❂   "
2.   The NCVS is based on a nationally representative sample of households and uses uniform procedures to select and interview respondents, thus enhancing the reliability of crime measures.
3.   Since individual people living in households are interviewed, the NCVS can be used in studies where ❂ ❂ ❂   .

B.   However, the NCVS cannot measure all crimes, in part because of procedures used to select victims.

1.   Since the survey is based on a sample of households, it cannot count crimes where ❂ ❂ ❂   .
2.   Victim surveys are not good measures of victimless crimes, since the individual survey respondents can't easily be conceived as victims.
3.   Measuring certain forms of delinquency through victim surveys presents similar problems.

C.   Since the NCVS, by design, excludes many types of crimes, you should recognize potential validity problems.

D.   What about the reliability of crime surveys in general and the NCVS in particular?

    1.   Since it is a survey, the NCVS is subject to the errors and shortcomings associated with that method of measuring concepts.

    2.   Asking people about crime brings up the possibility of different types of recall error.

    3.   Since the NCVS tries to count crimes that occur every six months, forward or backward ❂ ❂ ❂   can produce unreliable counts.

    4.   A different type of recall problem affects people who have been victimized several times over the six-month reference period (*series victimizations*).

    5.   Finally, the NCVS underestimates incidents where the victim and offender know each other—domestic violence or other assaults involving friends or acquaintances, for example.

XIV.   *NCVS Redesign*

A.   To address several concerns the NCVS has undergone substantial changes in the last several years. Victimization estimates from interviews conducted in 1993 reflect the full scope of the redesign effort after various changes in survey procedures were gradually incorporated.

    1.   For the most part, the redesign effort has focused on obtaining better measures of domestic violence and sexual assault, together with steps to help respondents recall a broader range of incidents.

    2.   Actual crime counts from the major changes in NCVS procedures have only recently become available, but early results indicate that the redesign has measured a greater number of incidents, especially ❂ ❂ ❂   .

B.   The redesigned NCVS has produced changes in crime counts for other offenses as well; the nature of these will become better known as researchers analyze the new survey data in more detail. However, there are two general points about the redesign and the NCVS in general that are important to recognize:

    1.   First, what you learn about crime from the NCVS or any other survey depends on ❂ ❂ ❂   .

    2.   The second is a consequence of the first: because of the redesigned NCVS, any effort to compare trends and changes in crime over time must take account of changes in measurement.

XV.   *Comparing Victim Surveys and Crimes Known to Police*

   A.   Researchers have devoted special attention to comparing data from the UCR and NCVS, in efforts to determine how the two measures differ and the strengths and weaknesses of each method for measuring crime.

      1.   In fact, Blumstein, Cohen, and Rosenfeld (1991:237) claim that "criminal justice researchers and policy analysts are fortunate in having two independent data series."
      2.   An early study by Skogan (1974) recognizes that crime surveys and police data take fundamentally different approaches to measuring crime, but that UCR and NCVS counts of robbery and auto theft are moderately related.

XVI.   *Surveys of Offending*

   A.   Just as survey techniques can measure crime by asking people to describe their experience as victims, people can also be asked about crimes they may have committed.

      1.   You might initially be skeptical of this technique: How truthful are people when asked about crimes they may have committed? Your concern would be well taken.
      2.   Self-report surveys, however, are probably the best method for trying to measure certain crimes that are ⦿ ⦿ ⦿   .
      3.   Crimes such as prostitution and drug abuse are excluded from victim surveys and underestimated by police measures of people arrested for these offenses.
      4.   A third class of offenses that might be better counted by self-report surveys are crimes that are rarely reported to police or observed by police. We mentioned shoplifting as one example.

XVII.   *National Household Survey on Drug Abuse*

   A.   Like the NCVS, the National Household Survey on Drug Abuse (NHSDA) is based on a ⦿ ⦿ ⦿   .

      1.   Both surveys are designed to monitor ⦿ ⦿ ⦿   .
      2.   Unlike the victimization survey, the central purpose of the NHSDA is to obtain self-reports of ⦿ ⦿ ⦿   .
      3.   The survey has been conducted since 1971 in various forms, though sampling and questioning procedures have been revised a few times.

4. The drug use survey includes questions to distinguish *lifetime* use (ever used) of different drugs from *current* use (used within the last month) and *heavy* use (used within the last week).

B. You should be able to recognize two potential sources of measurement problems with the NHSDA as we have briefly described the survey.

1. Do people tell the truth when asked about drug use?
2. The NHSDA incorporates certain procedures to encourage candid responses from individuals.
3. These procedures have been found to produce better measures of drug use than interviews conducted by telephone.
4. In fact, the circumstances of the NHSDA interview appear to especially affect ❂ ❂ ❂   .
5. The second problem arises because a household survey on drug use excludes people who do not live in traditional households.
6. In an effort to address this problem, beginning in 1991 the NHSDA surveys took special steps to include residents of college dorms, rooming houses, and homeless shelters.

XVIII. *Monitoring the Future*

A. Since 1975, the National Institute on Drug Abuse has sponsored an annual survey of high school seniors, Monitoring the Future: A Continuing Study of the Lifestyles and Values of Youth, or Monitoring the Future (MTF), for short.

1. The MTF survey is intended to monitor behaviors, ❂ ❂ ❂   ,
   .
2. The MTF actually includes several samples of high school students and others, totaling about 50,000 respondents each year (National Institute on Drug Abuse, 1996).
3. Each spring, high schools are sampled within particular ❂ ❂ ❂   .
4. Sampled students fill out computer scan sheets in response to batteries of questions that include self-reported use of ❂ ❂ ❂
   .
5. Respondents also report on involvement in delinquency and certain other illegal acts.
6. In addition, the MTF has expanded its samples over the years to include public school students in eighth and tenth grades (since 1991).
7. A subset of about 2,400 MTF respondents from the high school samples is selected each year to receive a follow-up mail questionnaire.
8. Each year both the MTF and NHSDA measure drug use for a *cross-section* of high school seniors and adults in households, providing a snapshot of annual rates of self-reported drug use.

9. Also note that examining annual results from MTF and the NHSDA over time provides *time series* or trend study that enables researchers and policy makers to detect changes in drug use among high school seniors, college students, and adults.

10. Finally, the follow-up samples of MTF respondents constitute a series of *panel studies* where changes in drug use among individual respondents can be ◐◐◐   .

XIX.   *Validity and Reliability of Self-report Measures*

A. A few quality studies have compared self-reported offending to other measures, usually records of offending from law enforcement and juvenile justice agencies.

◇   You may recognize this as an example of ◐◐◐   .

B. In a more recent longitudinal study of a sample of Pittsburgh youths, Farrington and associates (1996) examine convergent validity by again comparing self-reported offending and arrests to official records of arrests and juvenile petitions.

◇   Because it is a longitudinal panel study, interviewing the sample at multiple time points, the authors are able to estimate *predictive validity* by comparing self-reported delinquency at one time period to arrests and juvenile petitions at later times.

XX.   *Self-Report Surveys Summarized*

◇   Researchers and policymakers are best advised to be *critical users* of measures obtained from self-report surveys. Notice that we emphasize both "critical" and "users," meaning that self-reports can and should be used to measure offending, but that researchers, public officials, and others who use such measures should be aware of their strengths and limits.

1. Since MTF and NHSDA sampling and interviewing procedures have remained relatively constant, the surveys provide reasonably consistent information on trends in drug use or offending over time.

2. These two surveys are better as measures of change than as measures of ◐◐◐   .

3. Also consider the fact that alternative measures of offenses such as drug use and delinquency are not readily available.

XXI.   *Drug Surveillance Systems*

◇   The challenge of developing reliable and valid measures of such offenses as drug use has prompted researchers and policy makers to search for alternative approaches.

XXII.   *Drug Use Forecasting*

A.   The National Institute of Justice (NIJ) has conducted the Drug Use Forecasting (DUF) program since 1987.

1.   Four times per year, cities participating in DUF select samples of persons ❶❷❸

2.   Anonymous interviews and urine specimens are obtained from persons who agree to participate in the voluntary study.

3.   In 1995, about 225 adult males were selected in each of 23 participating cities; about 100 adult females were also selected in most sites, and samples of juvenile detainees were obtained from 12 cities.

4.   The main purpose of DUF is to provide an ongoing assessment of the prevalence of drug use among persons arrested for criminal offenses.

5.   Annual DUF results are widely distributed by NIJ and have come to be viewed as a rough and ready indicator of drug use among criminal offenders.

6.   An interesting aspect of DUF is the fact that it ❶❷❸

B.   In what ways is the DUF program selective as a measure of drug use?

1.   First, DUF operates in only ❶❷❸

2.   Second, and perhaps most important, is that DUF includes ❶❷❸

3.   Third, we noted that DUF interviews and testing are voluntary. Perhaps surprisingly, a large proportion of 1995 arrestees agreed to participate: over ❶❷❸

4.   Individual cities receive detailed guidelines on selecting participants, but selection procedures are neither random nor regularly monitored.

XXIII. *Drug Abuse Warning Network*

    ◇   The Drug Abuse Warning Network (DAWN) collects emergency medical treatment reports for "drug episodes" from a sample of ● ● ●

    1.   Drug episodes are defined as visits to a hospital emergency room that are produced by or directly related to use of illegal drugs, or non-medical use of legal drugs.

    2.   Notice that DAWN is based on units of analysis that are only indirectly linked to criminal offenses.

    3.   Since it was begun in the early 1970s, DAWN affords a comparatively long-term time series that monitors the most serious medical consequences of drug use. Like DUF, DAWN is best suited for measuring trends.

    4.   Like DUF, DAWN records include demographic and other information about the individuals whose drug episodes bring them ● ● ●

    5.   But the unusual unit of analysis for DAWN means that one individual can account for multiple drug episodes.

    6.   Mieczkowski (1996:387) points out that DAWN data for a single metropolitan area might serve as indicators of anti-drug program impact.

XIV. *Pulse Check*

    ◇   A recent addition to the battery of systems monitoring drug problems is completely different. Since 1992, the Office of National Drug Control Policy (ONDCP) has published a quarterly or semiannual report based on qualitative information obtained from selected cities.

    1.   *Pulse Check* reports efforts by researchers to collect information from three types of sources: ethnographers, local and federal law enforcement officers, and ● ● ● (ONDCP, 1996).

    2.   Researchers conduct semi-structured interviews by telephone, asking about trends in availability and use of different types of drugs.

    3.   The basic premise of ethnographic research is that researchers can learn much about social phenomena by ● ● ●

    4.   Similar semi-structured telephone interviews are conducted with police officers active in drug enforcement.

XXV. *Measuring Crime for Specific Purposes*

A. Each of the crime measures discussed so far can be used for a variety of research purposes—exploration, description, explanation and applied research. However each has the primary purpose of providing some type of crime count—crimes known to police, victimizations of households and people living in households, self-reported drug use and other offending, drug use among arrestees and emergency room patients, or qualitative assessments of drug use and availability in specific urban areas.

B. At this point we want to call your attention to examples of crime measures developed for specific research and policy purposes.

   1. **Crime Surveys** are especially useful ❂ ❂ ❂

   2. Because of the potential strengths of victim surveys it's becoming increasingly common for them to be conducted in specific states, cities, or even neighborhoods.

   3. **Incident-based Crime Records.** We mentioned earlier that larger jurisdictions have been slow to convert from UCR reporting to the NIBRS system, largely because police departments in large cities have tailored data management systems to their own needs.

   4. **Observing Crime.** We have mentioned that police learn about certain types of crime primarily through observation.

C. Notice certain things these examples of directed observation have in common.

   1. First, each has a fairly specific research or policy purpose. Baumer and Rosenbaum wanted to obtain estimates of shoplifting frequency and evaluate the effects of certain security measures; Homel and associates wished to learn more about the association between public drinking and violence; members of community organizations participate in neighborhood surveillance to take action against local drug and other problems.

   2. Second, the three examples focus on relatively small areas—a single department store, a sample of bars in Sydney, or a specific neighborhood.

   3. Finally, the expected density of incidents made observation an appropriate way to measure crime.

XXVI.   Measuring Crime: Summary

◇   Figure 6-4 summarizes some of what we have considered in this chapter by comparing the different measures of crime. Each method has its strengths and weaknesses.

1.   The UCR and SHR provide the best count for murder and crimes where the victim is either a ❂❂❂   .
2.   Crimes against persons or households that are not reported to police are best counted by the NCVS.
3.   Compared to the UCR, NIBRS potentially adds much greater detail to a much broader range of offenses.
4.   Self-report surveys are best at measuring crimes that do not have readily identifiable victims and those that ❂❂❂
5.   Sentinel measures target more narrowly defined populations and are best seen as measures of change.
6.   Don't forget that all crime measures are selective, and because of this it's critical that you understand the selection process.

KEY NAMES AND TERMS

Supplementary Homicide Reports (SHR)   Uniform Crime Reports (UCR)
Cross-section   National Incident-Based Reporting System (NIBRS)
Time series   National Crime Victimization Survey (NCVS)
Panel studies   National Household Survey on Drug Abuse
Pulse Check   Monitoring the Future (MTF)
Drug Use Forecasting (DUF)   Drug Abuse Warning Network (DAWN)

Multiple Choice Questions

1. While using crime as a dependent variable is criminal justice research, explanatory studies frequently seek to

    a. explain why crime is an important dependent variable.
    b. learn what causes crime.
    c. learn why criminal justice researchers depend on this variable to the degree that they do.
    d. all of the above.

2. Criminal justice researchers have used the variable "crime" in which of the following ways?

    a. explanatory studies
    b. exploratory studies
    c. descriptive studies
    d. all of the above

3. Once the decision to measure crime has been made, which of the following should be the next consideration?

    a. what the researcher is attempting to show through the research
    b. how the analysis will be conducted
    c. what offenses should be included in the measurement
    d. the potential threats to internal validity

4. Which of the following is an appropriate unit of analysis when measuring the concept of crime?

    a. the offender
    b. the victim
    c. offenses
    d. all of the above

5. The Uniform Crime Reports have been the basic official measure of crime since

    a. 1900
    b. 1930
    c. 1950
    d. 1976

6. One serious criticism of the UCR has been

    a. the 1976 decision to separate crimes into part I and part II crimes.
    b. the issue of whether police departments are the best source of official statistics
    c. the fact that is does not even try to count all crimes reported to the police.
    d. all of the above.

7. The most recent development in police-based measures at the national level is the ongoing effort by the FBI and the bureau of Justice Statistics to

    a. include more offenses in the UCR
    b. eliminate any distinctions between part I and part II offenses.
    c. add terrorism to the list of part I offenses
    d. convert the UCR to a National Incident-Based Reporting System.

8. By eliminating the hierarchy rule, the National Incident-Based Reporting System, means that

    a. only the most serious crime will be counted within any particular criminal incident.
    b. offense classifications are mutually exclusive.
    c. compared to the traditional UCR, fewer crimes should be counted on a national level.
    d. all of the above.

9. The National Crime Victimization Survey has been conducted since

    a. 1900
    b. 1930
    c. 1972
    d. 1990

10. Which of the following data collection efforts has been used to monitor drug use of American arrestee's.

    a. UCR
    b. NCVS
    c. MTF
    d. DUF

11.   _____ collects emergency medical treatment reports for "drug episodes" from a sample of over 500 hospitals and about 150 medical examiners nationwide.

   a.   UCR
   b.   Pulse Check
   c.   DAWN
   d.   DUF

12.   Since 1992, the Office of National Drug Control Policy has published a quarterly or semiannual report based on qualitative information obtained from selected cities called Pulse Check. This source is based on which of the following forms of data collection.

   a.   qualitative data: ethnographers, local and federal law enforcement officers, and drug treatment service providers.
   b.   qualitative data: interviews, focus groups, and participant observations
   c.   quantitative data: surveys, questionnaires, and police records
   d.   quantitative data: police records, correctional data, probation and parole surveys.

13.   Crime surveys are especially useful for

   a.   police departments to reorganize their organizational protocols
   b.   learning about crimes not reported to police.
   c.   learning about crimes reported to police
   d.   learning about the cost of crime on a national level

True/False Questions

1.   Crime is a fundamental dependent variable for criminal justice and criminology.

   a.   true
   b.   false

2.   Explanatory studies frequently focus on what actions might be effective in reducing crime, while applied studies seek to learn what causes crime.

   a.   true
   b.   false

3.   Descriptive and exploratory studies may simply wish to count how much crime there is in some specific area.

   a.   true
   b.   false

4. There is agreement among researchers and society alike with respect to the meaning of the concept "crime".

    a. true
    b. false

5. Organizations can not be used as a unit of analysis because organizations are made up of individuals, which would be the true unit of analysis.

    a. true
    b. false

6. The most widely used measure of crime are based on police records.

    a. true
    b. false

7. The Federal Bureau of Investigations has collected data for the National Criminal Victimization Survey since 1930.

    a. true
    b. false

8. The Supplementary Homicide Reports (SHR) are an example of data collected which are based on incidents of crime.

    a. true
    b. false

9. It is generally believed that the UCR has greatly enhanced the data collection procedure known as the National Incident-Based Reporting System.

    a. true
    b. false

10. Since 1975, the national Institute on Drug Abuse has sponsored an annual survey of high school seniors called "Monitoring the Future: A Continuing Study of the Lifestyles and Values of Youth.

    a. true
    b. false

Essay Questions

1. Describe the procedures traditionally used by the FBI to collect data for the Uniform Crime Reports. Continue by identifying the crimes classified as Part I offenses. Next, discuss three sources of measurement error associated with the traditional procedures used to construct the UCR. Finally, discuss the recent development to convert the UCR to a National Incident-Based Reporting System (NIBRS), as well as the specific shortcomings that are hoped to be addressed by such improvements.

2. Discuss the three purposes of measurement as described by the authors. Provide examples of each that have the potential to improve the surrounding community. After stating how the community could be improved through some form of measurement, select one form of data collection procedure presently funded by the United States Government which would address one of the identified purposes of measurement.

Chapter 7

EXPERIMENTAL AND QUASI-EXPERIMENTAL DESIGNS

Chapter Outline

I. *Introduction*

♦ We first discuss the *experiment* as "a process of observation, to be carried out in a situation expressly brought about for that purpose." At base, experiments involve (1) taking action and (2) ❍ ❍ ❍

1. Social scientific researchers typically select a group of subjects, do something to them, and observe the effect of what was done.
2. It is worth noting at the outset that experiments also are often used in nonscientific human inquiry.

II. *Topics Appropriate to Experiments*

♦ Experiments are especially well suited to research projects ❍ ❍ ❍

1. Experimentation, then, is especially appropriate for ❍ ❍ ❍
2. Because experiments are best suited for hypothesis testing, they may also be appropriate in the study of criminal justice policy.
3. You might typically think of experiments being conducted in laboratories, however, criminal justice experiments are almost always conducted in field settings, ❍ ❍ ❍

III. *The Classical Experiment*

♦ The most conventional type of experiment, in the natural as well as social sciences, involves three major pairs of components:

1. independent and dependent variables
2. ❍ ❍ ❍
3. experimental and control groups

IV.   *Independent and Dependent Variables*

A.   Typically, the independent variable takes the form of an experimental stimulus, which is either present or absent—that is, a dichotomous variable, having two attributes.

1.   The independent and dependent variables appropriate to experimentation are ◐◐◐   .

2.   It should be noted, moreover, that a given variable might serve as an independent variable in one experiment and as ◐◐◐
.

B.   In the terms of our earlier discussion of cause and effect, the independent variable is the cause and the dependent variable is the effect.

C.   It is essential that both independent and dependent variables ◐◐◐
.

◇   Conventionally, in the experimental model, dependent and independent variables must be operationally defined before the experiment begins.

V.   *Pretesting and Posttesting*

◇   In the simplest experimental design, subjects are measured in terms of a dependent variable (pretested), exposed to a stimulus representing an independent variable, and then ◐◐◐   (posttested).

◇   Differences noted between the first and second measurements on the dependent variable are then attributed to the influence of the independent variable.

VI.   *Experimental and Control Groups*

A.   The foremost method of offsetting the effects of the experiment itself is the use of a ◐◐◐   .

1.   Laboratory experiment seldom, if ever, involve only the observation of an experimental group to which a stimulus has been administered.

2.   The researchers also observe a control group to which the experimental stimulus has ◐◐◐   .

3.   Using a control group allows the researcher to control for the effects of the experiment itself.

B. The need for control groups in social research became clear in connection with a series of studies of employee satisfaction conducted by F. J. Roethlisberger and W. J. Dickson (1939) in the late 1920s and early 1930s.

    1. These two researchers studied working conditions in the telephone "bank wiring room" of Western Electric Works in Chicago, attempting to discover what changes in working conditions would improve employee ◐◐◐   .

    2. To the researchers' great satisfaction, they discovered that making working conditions better consistently increased satisfaction and productivity.

    3. As the workroom was brightened up through better lighting, for example, productivity ◐◐◐   .

    4. To further substantiate their scientific conclusion, the researchers then dimmed the lights: *productivity again improved!*

    5. It became evident then that the wiring room workers were responding more to the attention given them by the researchers than to improved working conditions. As a result of this phenomenon, often called the *Hawthorne effect,* ◐◐◐

        .

C. In criminal justice experiments, control groups are important as a guard not only against the effects of the experiments themselves but also against the effects of events that may occur outside the laboratory during the course of experiments.

VII. Double-Blind Experiment

◇ In medical research, the experiments may be more likely to "observe" improvements among patients receiving the experimental drug than among those receiving the ◐◐◐   .

    1. A double-blind experiment eliminates that possibility, because neither the subjects nor the experimenters know which is the experimental group and which the control.

    2. In the medical case, those researchers who were responsible for administering the drug and for noting improvements would not be told which subjects were receiving the drug and which were receiving the placebo.

VIII. Selecting Subjects

◇ Before beginning an experiment, you must make two basic decisions about who will participate.

1. First, you must decide on the target population—the group to which the results of your experiment will apply.
2. The second step is to decide ◐ ◐ ◐

3. Aside from the question of generalizability, the cardinal rule of subject selection and experimentation concerns the comparability of experimental and control groups.
4. It is essential, therefore, that experimental and control groups be ◐ ◐ ◐
.

IX. Randomization

◇ **Randomization** is a central feature of the classical experiment. The most important characteristic of randomization is that it produces experimental and control groups that are ◐ ◐ ◐ .

◇ Randomization insures that the average unit in [the] treatment group is approximately equivalent to the average unit in another [group] before the treatment is applied.

X. Experiments and Causal Inference

◇ The central features of the classical experiment are independent and dependent variables, pretesting and posttesting, and experimental and control groups, ideally created through random assignment.

1. Think of these features as building blocks of a research design to demonstrate a ◐ ◐ ◐ .
2. The experimental design ensures that the *cause precedes the effect in time* by taking posttest measurements of the dependent variable after introducing the experimental stimulus.
3. The second criterion for causation, an *empirical correlation between the cause-and-effect variables*, is determined ◐ ◐ ◐
.
4. A change from pretest to posttest measures demonstrates ◐ ◐ ◐ .

XI. Threats to Internal Validity

◇ The problem of internal invalidity refers to the possibility that the conclusions drawn from experimental results may not accurately reflect what has gone on in the experiment itself.

1. ***History***. Historical events may occur during the course of the experiment that will ◐◑◒ .
2. ***Maturation***. People are continually growing and changing, whether in an experiment or not, and those changes affect the results of the experiment.
3. ***Testing***. Often the process of testing and retesting will influence people's behavior, thereby confounding the experimental results.
4. ***Instrumentation***. Is concerned with changes in the measurement process itself, and ◐◑◒ .
5. ***Statistical regression***. Sometimes it's appropriate to conduct experiments on subjects who start out with extreme scores on the dependent variable. However, it is important to understand that even without any experimental stimulus, the group as a whole is likely to show some improvement over time. Commonly referred to as regression to the mean, this validity threat can emerge whenever researchers are interested in cases that have extreme scores on some variable.
6. ***Selection biases***. Randomization eliminates the potential for systematic bias in selecting subjects, but subjects ◐◑◒ .
7. ***Experimental mortality***. Often, experimental subjects will drop out of the experiment before it is completed, and the statistical comparisons and conclusions drawn can be affected by that.
8. ***Causal time order***. In criminal justice research, there is often a possibility of ambiguity about the time order of the experimental stimulus and the dependent variable. Whenever this occurs, the research conclusion that the stimulus caused the dependent variable can be challenged with the explanation that the "dependent" variable actually caused changes in the stimulus.
9. ***Diffusion or imitation of treatments***. In the event that experimental and control-group subjects are in communication with each other, it's possible that experimental subjects will pass on some elements of the experimental stimulus to the control group.
10. ***Compensatory treatment***. In experiments in real-life situations subjects in the control group are often deprived of something considered to be of value. In such cases, there may ◐◑◒ .
11. ***Compensatory rivalry***. In real-life experiments, the subjects deprived of the experimental stimulus may try to compensate for the missing stimulus by working harder.
12. ***Demoralization***. Feelings of deprivation among the control group may ◐◑◒ .
13. Notice that the possibilities of compensatory rivalry and demoralization are based on subjects' reactions to the experiment, while diffusion and compensatory treatment are accidental or intentional extensions of the experimental stimulus to the control group.

XII.   Ruling Out Threats to Internal Validity

✦   The classical experiment, if coupled with proper subject selection and assignment, can *potentially* handle each of the 12 threats to internal validity.

1. "Estimating the internal validity of a relationship is a deductive process in which the investigator has to systematically think through how each of the internal validity threats can be ruled out."
2. We emphasize careful administration here. Random assignment, pretest and posttest measures, or using control and experimental groups cannot ❂ ❂ ❂   .
3. This caution is especially true in field studies and evaluation research, where subjects participate in natural settings and uncontrolled variation in the experimental stimulus may be present.
4. Field experiments and evaluations can present many obstacles that are not eliminated by simply adopting a randomized experimental design. Careful administration and control, throughout the experiment, are necessary to reduce potential threats to internal validity.

XIII.   Generalizability

✦   In addition to problems of validity, there are problems of generalizing from experimental findings to ❂ ❂ ❂   .

1. Even if the results of an experiment are an accurate gauge of what happened during that experiment, do they really tell us anything about life in the wilds of society?
2. We will consider two dimensions of generalizability: construct validity and ❂ ❂ ❂   .

XIV.   Threats to Construct Validity

A.   In the language of experimentation, construct validity is the correspondence between the empirical test of a hypothesis and the underlying causal process that the experiment is intended to represent.

✦   Construct validity is concerned with generalizing from what we observe in an experiment to ❂ ❂ ❂   .

B.   Almost any empirical example or measure of a construct will be ❶ ❷ ❸ .

         1.   Part of construct validity refers to how completely an empirical measure can represent a construct, or how well you can generalize from a measure to a construct.

         2.   A related issue in construct validity is whether a given level of treatment is sufficient.

C.   Threats to construct validity present difficulty problems in criminal justice experiments, often because researchers are not clear in specifying precisely what constructs are to be represented by specific measures or experimental treatments.

        ◇   David Farrington and associates (1986:92) make a related point: "Most treatments in existing experiments are not based on a well-developed theory but on a vague idea about what might influence offending. The treatments given are often heterogeneous, making it difficult to know which element was responsible for any observed effect."

D.   Three elements of enhancing construct validity, therefore, are:

         1.   linking constructs and measures to ❶ ❷ ❸
         2.   clearly indicating what constructs are represented by specific measures
         3.   thinking carefully about what levels of treatment may be necessary to produce some level of change in the dependent measure.

XV.   *Threats to External Validity*

A.   Will an experimental study, conducted with the kind of control we have emphasized here, produce results that would also be found in more natural settings?

        ◇   Threats to external validity are greater for experiments conducted under ❶ ❷ ❸ .

B.   There is, however, a fundamental conflict between internal and external validity.

         1.   Threats to internal validity are reduced by conducting experiments under carefully controlled conditions, which may restrict our ability to generalize results to real-world settings.
         2.   Field experiments generally have greater external validity, but internal validity may suffer because such studies are more difficult to monitor than those taking place in more controlled settings.

C. Cook and Campbell (1979:83) offer some useful advice in trying to resolve the potential for conflict between ❂ ❂ ❂.

    1. Explanatory studies that test cause-and-effect theories should place greater emphasis on internal validity, while applied studies should be more concerned with external validity.

    2. This is not a hard-and-fast rule, since internal validity must be established before external validity becomes an issue.

XVI. Threats to Statistical Conclusions Validity

A. Virtually all experimental research in criminal justice is based on samples of subjects that represent a ❂ ❂ ❂.

B. Larger samples of subjects, up to a point, are more representative of the target population than are smaller samples.

C. Statistical conclusion validity becomes an issue when findings are based on small samples of cases.

    1. Because experiments are often costly and time consuming, they are frequently conducted with relatively small numbers of subjects.

    2. In such cases, only large differences between experimental and control groups on posttest measures can be detected with any degree of confidence.

XVII. Variations in the Classical Experimental Design

A. We now turn to a more systematic consideration of variations on the classical experiment that can be produced by manipulating the building blocks of experiments. There are four basic building blocks in experimental designs:

    1. the number of experimental and control groups
    2. the number and variation of ❂ ❂ ❂
    3. the number of pretest and posttest measurements
    4. the procedures used to select subjects and assign them to groups
    5. In general, posttest designs are appropriate when researchers suspect that the process of measurement may bias subjects' responses to a questionnaire or other instrument.

B. Figure 7-3 also shows a factorial design, with two experimental groups that receive different treatments, or different levels of a single treatment, and one control group.

1. This design is useful for comparing the effects of different interventions, or different amounts of a single treatment.
2. Thus, an experimental design may have more than one group receiving different versions or levels of experimental treatment.
3. We can also vary the number of measurements made on dependent variables.
4. However, a useful rule of thumb is to keep a design as simple as possible to control plausible threats to validity.

XVIII. Quasi-Experimental Designs

A. By now you should recognize the value of random assignment in controlling threats to validity.

   1. However, it is often not possible to randomly select subjects for experimental and control groups.
   2. There may be legal or ethical reasons why randomization cannot be used in criminal justice experiments.

B. When randomization is not possible, the next best choice is often a *quasi-experimental* design.

   1. The prefix *quasi-* is significant, meaning "❶ ❷ ❸   ."
   2. In most cases, quasi-experiments lack random assignment of subjects and therefore may be subject to the internal validity threats that are so well controlled in true experiments.
   3. Following Cook and Campbell, we will group quasi-experimental designs into two categories: nonequivalent-groups designs and ❶ ❷ ❸   .

XIX. Nonequivalent-Groups Designs

A. We assume that random assignment produces experimental and control groups that are equivalent. When it is not possible to create groups through randomization, we must use some other procedure, one that is not random. But if we construct groups through some non-random procedure, we cannot assume that the groups will be equivalent, hence the label *nonequivalent-groups design*.

   1. Whenever experimental and control groups are not equivalent, we should take care to select subjects in some way that makes the two groups as comparable as possible.
   2. Often the experimental group are matched against subjects in a comparison group.

B. You may be wondering how a researcher selects important variables to use in matching experimental and comparison subjects.

    1. We cannot give you a definitive answer to that question, any more than we could specify what particular variables should be used in any given experiment.

    2. The answer, ultimately, depends on the ⦾ ⦾ ⦾

    3. As a general rule, however, the two groups should be comparable in terms of variables likely to be related to the dependent variable under study.

    4. Experimental and comparison groups that match individual subjects is referred to as ⦾ ⦾ ⦾

    5. It is also possible to construct experimental and comparison groups through *aggregate matching*, where average characteristics of each group are comparable.

C. Deterring Obscene Phone Calls. In 1988, the New Jersey Bell telephone company introduced caller identification and instant call tracing in a small number of telephone exchange areas.

    1. Ronald Clarke (1992) studied the effects of these new technologies in deterring obscene phone calls.

    2. Clarke expected that obscene calls would decline in areas where the new services were available.

    3. After one year, formal complaints had declined sharply from areas serviced by the new technology, while no decline was found in other New Jersey Bell areas.

D. Three studies were used [in the textbook] to illustrate different approaches to research design when it is possible to randomly assign subjects to treatment and control groups.

    ✧ Lacking random assignment, it is necessary to use creative procedures for selecting subjects, constructing treatment and comparison groups, measuring dependent variables, and exercising other controls to reduce possible validity threats.

XX. *Cohort Designs*

    ✧ Recall that a cohort may be defined ⦾ ⦾ ⦾

◇ Groups are not equivalent, since they were not created by random assignment, but if we could assume that a comparison cohort did not systematically differ from a treatment cohort on important variables, we would be able to. . .

XXI. Time-Series Designs

A. Time-series designs are common examples of longitudinal studies in criminal justice research.

◇ A time-series design involves examining a series of observations on some variable over time.

B. An *interrupted time series* is a special type of time-series design that can be used in cause-and-effect studies.

1. A series of observations is compared before and after some intervention has been introduced.
2. Interrupted time series designs can be very useful in criminal justice research, especially in ❶ ❷ ❸   .
3. An important limit to interrupted time-series designs is that they operationalize complex causal constructs in simple ways.

C. Instrumentation can be a particular problem in time-series designs for two reasons.

1. First, observations are usually made over a relatively long time period, increasing the likelihood that changes in measurement instruments will occur.
2. Second, time-series designs often use measures that are produced by an organization such as a police department, criminal court, probation office, or corrections department.

XXII. Variations in Time-Series Designs

A. If we view the basic interrupted time-series design as an adaptation of basic design building blocks, we can consider how modifications can help control many validity problems.

1. The simplest time-series design studies one group, the treatment group, over time.
2. But rather than making one pretest and posttest observation, a longer series of observations are made before and after introducing an experimental treatment.

3. A single-series design may be modified by introducing and ❂❂❂

XXIII. *Experimental and Quasi-Experimental Designs Summarized*

A. By now, we hope you recognize that there are no magic formulas or cookbooks for designing an experimental or quasi-experimental study.

1. Researchers have an almost infinite variety of ways of varying the number and composition of groups of subjects, selecting subjects, determining how many observations to make, and deciding on what types of experimental stimuli to introduce or study.
2. This chapter has focused on variations in experimental and quasi-experimental designs, but there are other ways to structure research.
3. Even when experimental designs would be the best choice, it is not always possible to construct treatment and control groups, to utilize random assignment, or even to analyze a series of observations over time.

B. Experiments are best suited to topics ❂❂❂

1. Experiments and quasi-experiments also require that researchers be able to exercise, or at least approximate, some degree of control over an experimental stimulus.
2. Finally, these designs depend on being able to unambiguously establish the time order of experimental treatments and observations on the dependent variable.
3. Often, it is not possible to ❂❂❂

C. In designing a research project, you should always be alert to opportunities for using an experimental design.

1. You should also be aware of how various quasi-experimental designs can be developed when ❂❂❂
2. Experiments and quasi-experiments lend themselves to a logical rigor that is often much more difficult to achieve in other modes of observation.

KEY NAMES AND TERMS

experiment	individual matching
independent variable	aggregate matching
dependent variable	interrupted time series
randomization	time-series design with switching replications
quasi-experimental	design with nonequivalent dependent variables

MULTIPLE CHOICE QUESTIONS

1. One important feature of classical experiments is

    a. randomization.
    b. being able to study a phenomenon over time.
    c. loose definitions of concepts and propositions.
    d. interviews to supplement survey information.

2. The following diagram is an example of which type of experimental design?

    O   O   X   O   O   O
    t1   t2   t3   t4   t5

    a. interrupted time series
    b. classical experiment
    c. quasi-experiment
    d. interrupted time series with switching replications

3. A group of 100 university students are randomly selected and assigned to either a control group or experimental group. Each group completes a survey on attitudes toward police. Members of the experimental group participate in ride-alongs with local police officers over the course of the next week, after which both groups complete a similar attitudinal survey. This is an example of which type of research design?

    a. interrupted time series design
    b. nonequivalent-groups design
    c. classical experimental design
    d. cohort design

4. A double-blind experiment is one in which

    a. the researcher and the subjects are unaware of which is the control group and which is the experimental group.
    b. both the control group and experimental group are unaware of the purpose of the study.
    c. both the control group and experimental group are unaware that they are being observed.
    d. placebos are provided to the control group and the experimental group.

5. A group of people are released from State Prison on July 1, 1994. These people have been selected to take part in a study regarding post-release employment, which consists of an interview one month after release. This is an example of which type of research design?

    a. classical experimental design.
    b. time-series design.
    c. cohort design.
    d. reliable design.

6. The following would be an example of which type of research design?

    O   O   O   X   O   O   O

    O   O   O   O   O   O
    t1   t2   t3   t4   t5   t6   t7

    a. simple interrupted time series.
    b. interrupted time series with nonequivalent comparison group.
    c. interrupted time series with removed treatment.
    d. interrupted time series with switching replications.

7. An experimental design would best be suited for which of the following research purposes?

    a. testing the hypothesis that viewing an educational video on AIDS will alter prostitutes' attitudes toward condom use
    b. determining the number of cities that have community policing
    c. describing the locations and types of violent crimes in a large city
    d. describing the racial composition of persons sentenced to death in the United States

8. Which one of the following is not one of the central features of the classical experiment?

    a. independent and dependent variables
    b. individual matching of subjects
    c. pretesting and posttesting
    d. experimental and control groups created through random assignment

9.   Threats to this type of validity become an issue when findings are based on relatively small numbers of subjects.

    a.   external validity
    b.   statistical conclusion validity
    c.   construct validity
    d.   face validity

10.   Which one of the following is not a possible threat to internal validity?

    a.   statistical regression
    b.   testing
    c.   maturation
    d.   theory

11.   Experimental mortality refers to

    a.   a need to discontinue the study due to a lack of funding.
    b.   a finding that your hypothesis was not supported by the results.
    c.   subjects dropping out of the experiment before it is completed.
    d.   death of the researcher.

12.   Diffusion of treatments refers to

    a.   a "contamination" of the control group due to communication between the experimental and control groups.
    b.   more than one treatment or stimulus applied to the experimental group.
    c.   continuation of treatments after conclusion of the experiment.
    d.   assignment of the experimental stimulus or treatment through randomization.

13.   Dr. Frankencrime conducted a year-long study of offender treatment in prison. Volunteer subjects were randomly assigned to either the experimental or control group. The subjects in the experimental group were administered electric shocks three times a day, while watching extremely violent videos. Members of the control group were administered the shocks without the videos. The good Doctor finds that by the end of the year, her original sample of 200 offenders has dropped to 50, due to the large number of subjects who quit the study early. This is an illustration of which one of the following threats to internal validity?

    a.   demoralization
    b.   history
    c.   statistical regression
    d.   experimental mortality

14. Which one of the following is not a strategy for dealing with threats to construct validity?

    a. linking constructs and measures to theory
    b. carefully considering the level of treatment necessary to produce some level of change in the dependent measure.
    c. shortening the time between pretest and posttest.
    d. clearly indicating what constructs are represented by specific measures.

15. A researcher is interested in studying the effect of parental divorce on late adolescent criminality. She wishes to compare teenagers whose parents had divorced at some point in their childhood, to teenagers whose parents remained married. The design most appropriate for this research idea is the

    a. classical experimental design.
    b. interrupted time-series design.
    c. double-blind experiment.
    d. nonequivalent-groups design.

True/False Questions

1. Fundamentally, experiments involve (1) taking action, and (2) observing the consequences of that action.

    a. true
    b. false

2. Experiments are especially well suited to research projects involving relatively well-defined concepts and propositions.

    a. true
    b. false

3. The component of all experiments, that distinguish them from all other research designs, is the presence of both a pretest and a posttest.

    a. true
    b. false

4. The independent and dependent variables appropriate to experimentation are nearly limitless.

    a. true
    b. false

5.   Conventionally, in the experimental model, dependent and independent variables must be operationally defined after the experiment begins, since the research is never sure of the best way to measure a variable until the experiment is underway.

        a.   true
        b.   false

6.   The foremost method of offsetting the effects of the experiment itself is the use of a control group.

        a.   true
        b.   false

7.   using a control group allows the researcher to control for the effects of the experiment itself.

        a.   true
        b.   false

8.   The Hawthorne effect is typically sought by researchers using the experimental design because a causal statement can be made.

        a.   true
        b.   false

9.   Selection bias is concerned with the most appropriate measurement devise selected for a given piece of research.

        a.   true
        b.   false

10.   Time-series designs are common examples of longitudinal studies in criminal justice research.

        a.   true
        b.   false

Essay Questions

1.   Describe the classical experiment, including the role of variables, pretesting and posttesting, experimental and control groups, and randomization. Finally, discuss four threats to internal validity and explain why the experimental design is a good design to help reduce the effects of such threats.

2.   Provide three criminal justice-related examples of topics for which a quasi-experimental design would be more appropriate to use than a classical experimental design. Explain why.

Chapter 8

ETHICS AND CRIMINAL JUSTICE RESEARCH

Chapter Outline

I. *Introduction*

      ◇   Ethical considerations represent a compromise in criminal justice research, somewhat subtle and less obvious, but nonetheless ❂ ❂ ❂   .

              1.   Just as you wouldn't use certain procedures because they are impractical or too expensive, so also are there procedures you couldn't use because of ethical considerations.

              2.   The problem in criminal justice research--and probably in life--is that ethical considerations ❂ ❂ ❂   .

II. *Ethical Issues in Criminal Justice Research*

      A.   In most dictionaries and in common usage, ethics is typically associated with morality, and both deal with matters of ❂ ❂ ❂   .

              1.   But what is right and what is wrong?
              2.   What is the source of the distinction?

      B.   *Webster's New World Dictionary* defines ethical as "conforming to the standards of conduct of ❂ ❂ ❂   ."

              1.   Although the idea may frustrate those in search of moral absolutes, what we regard as morality and ethics in day-to-day life is a matter of agreement among members of a group.

              2.   Not surprisingly, different groups have agreed ❂ ❂ ❂   .

              3.   If you are going to do criminal justice research, you should be aware of the general agreements shared by researchers about what's proper and improper in the conduct of scientific inquiry.

III.   *No Harm to Participants*

A.   Balancing the potential benefits from doing research against the possibility of harm to the people being studied--or harm to others--is a fundamental ethical dilemma in all research.

   ◇   Criminal justice research has the potential to produce physical and psychological harm, as well as ◉◉◉   .

B.   Although the likelihood of physical harm may seem remote, it is worthwhile to consider possible ways this might occur.

   1.   Harm to subjects, researchers, or third parties is a potential threat in field studies that collect information from or about persons engaged in criminal activity; this is especially true for field research.
   2.   Collecting information from active criminals presents at least the possibility of violence against research subjects by other drug dealers.

C.   Some potential for psychological harm to subjects exists when interviews are used to collect information.

   1.   Crime surveys that ask respondents about their experiences as victims of crime may remind them of a traumatic, or at least an unpleasant, experience.
   2.   Although the fact often goes unrecognized, subjects can be harmed by the analysis and reporting of data.

D.   By now, you should have realized that just about any research you might conduct runs some risk of injuring other people somehow.

   1.   A researcher can never completely guard against all these possible injuries.
   2.   Yet some study designs make such injuries more likely than others.
   3.   As a general principle, possible harm to subjects may be justified if the ◉◉◉   . Of course, this raises a further question of how you determine whether possible benefits offset possible harms.

IV.   *Voluntary Participation*

    A.   Criminal justice research often, though not always, represents an ◉ ◉ ◉
.

        ◇   Moreover, criminal justice research often requires that people reveal personal information about themselves--information ◉ ◉ ◉
.

    B.   A major tenet of medical research ethics is that experimental participation must be ◉ ◉ ◉
.

        ◇   The same norm applies to research in criminal justice. No one should be forced to participate.

    C.   You should be clear that this norm of voluntary participation goes directly against a number of scientific concerns.

        1.   The scientific goal of generalizability is threatened if experimental subjects or survey respondents are all the kinds of people who willingly participate in such things.
        2.   Often, a researcher conducting observations in the field cannot even reveal that a study is being done, for fear that that revelation might significantly affect what is being studied.
        3.   You should realize that the norm of voluntary participation is an important one, and you should also know that it is <u>sometimes</u> impossible to follow it.

V.   *Anonymity and Confidentiality*

    A.   **Anonymity** A survey respondent or other person being studied may be considered *anonymous* when the ◉ ◉ ◉

        1.   Anonymity takes care of ◉ ◉ ◉
.
        2.   Studies that use field observation techniques are often able to ensure that research subjects cannot be identified.
        3.   However, respondents in many surveys cannot be considered anonymous, since an interviewer collects the information from a person whose name and address may be known.
        4.   However, assuring anonymity makes it difficult to keep track of <u>completed interviews with sampled respondents.</u>
        5.   Despite this problem, there are some situations in which you may be advised to pay the necessary price.

B. Other situations that use data collected by other means may similarly make it impossible to guarantee anonymity for subjects.

C. **Confidentiality** *Confidentiality* means that a researcher is able to ◐ ◐ ◐ .

  ◇ In a survey of self-reported drug use, for example, the researcher would be in a position to make public the use of illegal drugs by a given respondent, but the respondent is assured that this will not be done.

D. You can use a number of techniques to ensure better performance on this guarantee.

  1. As soon as possible, all names and addresses should be removed from data-collection forms and ◐ ◐ ◐ .
  2. A master identification file should be created linking numbers to names to permit the later correction of missing or contradictory information.
  3. This file should be kept under lock and key and should be available only for legitimate purposes.
  4. Whenever a survey is confidential rather than anonymous, it is the researcher's responsibility to ◐ ◐ ◐ .
  5. In any event, subjects should be assured that information they provide will be used for research purposes only, and not be disclosed to third parties.

VI. *Deceiving Subjects*

  ◇ Handling your own identity as a researcher can be tricky also.

  1. Sometimes it's useful and even necessary to ◐ ◐ ◐ .

  2. Even when it's possible and important to conceal your research identity, there is an important ethical dimension to be considered.
  3. Deceiving people is unethical, and within criminal justice research, deception needs to be justified by compelling scientific or administrative concerns.

VII. *Analysis and Reporting*

A. As a criminal justice researcher, then, you have a number of ethical obligations to your subjects of study.

B. At the same time, you have ethical obligations to your ◐ ◐ ◐ .

1. You have an obligation to make any shortcomings of your research known to your readers.
2. Negative findings should be reported if they are at all related to your analysis.
3. You should avoid the temptation to save face by describing your findings as the product of a carefully preplanned analytic strategy when that is not the case.
4. You can serve your fellow researchers—and scientific discovery as a whole—by telling the truth about all the pitfalls and problems you have experienced in a particular line of inquiry.

VIII.   Legal Liability

◇   Two types of ethical problems expose researchers to potential legal liability.

1. Under criminal law in many states, you might be arrested for obstruction of justice, or being an accessory to a crime. Potentially more troublesome is the situation when participant observation of crime or deviance draws researchers into criminal or deviant roles themselves.
2. The more common potential source of legal problems is having knowledge that research subjects have committed illegal acts.
3. Or research data may be subject to subpoena by a criminal court. Since disclosure of research data that could be traced to individual subjects would violate the ethical principle of confidentiality, a new dilemma emerges.

IX.   Special Problems

A   Certain types of criminal justice studies may present particular ethical problems in addition to those we have already mentioned.

◇   *Staff Misbehavior*   In the course of conducting applied research, you may also become aware of irregular or illegal practices by staff in public agencies.

B.   **Research Causes Crime**   Because criminal acts and their circumstances are complex and imperfectly understood, there is sometimes a potential for a research project to produce crime, or influence its location or target. Needless to say, this represents ◉ ◉ ◉   .

◇   For example, how might subjects use cash payments they receive in exchange for being interviewed about drug use

C. A different type of ethical problem is the possibility of crime displacement in studies of crime prevention programs.

D. **Withholding Desirable Treatments** Experimental designs in criminal justice research can produce different kinds of ethical questions.

   1. Recall our discussion of compensatory threats to validity when a desirable treatment is provided to an experimental group and withheld from a control group.
   2. Failure to conduct research, even at the potential expense of control group subjects, would therefore make it ☼ ☼ ☼

   3. One solution to this dilemma is to interrupt an experiment if preliminary results indicate that a new policy, or drug, does in fact produce improvements in a treatment group.

E. **Random Assignment** The use of random assignment in experimental studies raises similar questions.

   1. If a desirable or beneficial policy is being tested, is it ethical to assign the treatment randomly to some people and not to others?
   2. Researchers, however, generally view random assignment as an ethical procedure for deciding how potentially beneficial (or harmful) experimental treatments should be allocated among subjects.

F. Research in criminal justice, especially applied research, can pose a variety of ethical dilemmas, only some of which we have mentioned here.

X. *Promoting Compliance with Ethical Principles*

A. But if the professionals who design and conduct a research project may fail to consider ethical problems, how can such problems be avoided?

   1. One approach is for researchers to consult one of ☼ ☼ ☼

   2. Formal codes of conduct describe what is considered acceptable and unacceptable professional behavior.

B. Professional codes of ethics for social scientists cannot, however, be expected to prevent unethical practices in criminal justice research any more than the American Bar Association's Code of Professional Responsibility eliminates breaches of ethics by attorneys.

XI.   *Institutional Review Boards*

A.   Government agencies and nongovernment organizations (including universities) that conduct research involving human subjects must establish review committees, known as institutional review boards (IRB). These IRBs have two general purposes.

   1.   First, board members make judgments about the overall risks to human subjects, and whether these risks are acceptable, given ❶❷❸

   2.   Second, the IRB determines whether procedures to be used by the project include adequate safeguards to protect the safety, confidentiality, and general welfare of human subjects.

   3.   It's safe to assume that most research is subject to IRB review if original data will be collected from individuals whose identities will be known.

B.   **Informed Consent** The norm of voluntary participation is usually satisfied by informing subjects about research procedures, ❶❷❸

   1.   Informed consent requires that subjects understand the purpose of research, possible risks and side effects, possible benefits to subjects, and ❶❷❸

   2.   Researchers usually address this problem by telling subjects part of the truth, or a slightly revised version of why the research is being conducted.

C.   Another potential problem with obtaining informed consent is ensuring that subjects have the capacity to understand your description of risks, benefits, procedures, and so forth.

   1.   You may have to provide oral descriptions to participants who are unable to read.

   2.   If you use specialized terms or language common in criminal justice research, participants may not understand your meaning and thus ❶❷❸

D.   It is important that you understand how informed consent addresses a variety of ethical issues in conducting criminal justice research.

   1.   First of all, it ensures that participation is voluntary.

   2.   Secondly, by informing subjects of procedures, risks, and benefits, you are empowering them to resolve the fundamental ethical dilemma of whether the possible benefits of the research offset the possible risks of participation

E.   **Special Populations** Federal regulations on human subjects include special provisions for certain types of subjects, two of which are particularly important in criminal justice research—juveniles and prisoners.

1.   Juveniles, of course, are treated differently from adults in most aspects of the law. Their status as a special population of human subjects reflects the legal status of juveniles, as well as their capacity to grant informed consent.

2.   Prisoners are treated as a special population for somewhat different reasons. Because of their ready accessibility for experiments and interviews, prisoners have been frequently used in biomedical experiments that produced serious harm to subjects.

3.   Recognizing this, HHS regulations specify that prisoner subjects may not be exposed to risks that would be considered excessive for nonprison subjects.

4.   Furthermore, undue influence or coercion cannot be used in recruiting prisoner subjects.

XII.   *Institutional Review Board Requirements and Researcher Rights*

◇   Federal regulations contain many more provisions for institutional review boards and other protections for human subjects.

1.   Some researchers may feel that such regulations actually *create* ethical problems by setting constraints on their freedom and professional judgments in conducting research.

2.   However, since researchers are not always disinterested parties in answering such questions, IRBs are established ◐ ◐ ◐

3.   Also recognize that IRBs can be sources of expert advice on ◐ ◐ ◐

XIII.   *Two Ethical Controversies*

XIV.   *Trouble in the Tearoom*

XV.   *Simulating a Prison*

KEY NAME AND TERMS

Anonymity	Voluntary participation
Confidentiality	Institutional Review Board
Ethics	Informed Consent

Multiple Choice Questions

1. One ethical issue in criminal justice research is not to harm participants in the study. This includes

   a. not harming the people being studied.
   b. not harming researchers involved in the study.
   c. not harming the research institution's reputation.
   d. only a and b are included in the no harm to participants issue.

2. According to the text, IRB stands for

   a. inter-rater believability
   b. illogical reasoning bias
   c. institutional review board
   d. injustice rule book

3. Harm to research participants can include which of the following?

   a. embarrassment
   b. psychological harm
   c. physical harm
   d. all of the above

4. A researcher hypothesizes that low intelligence is a significant risk factor for delinquency. However, he unexpectedly finds that school achievement cancels out the relationship between IQ and delinquency; there is no direct relationship between intelligence and delinquent behavior. Ethical principles would suggest that the researcher take which one of the following courses of action?

   a. Report that he expected the relationship between school achievement and delinquency from the onset of the study.
   b. Fail to report any findings at all, since his original hypothesis was not supported.
   c. Report that he unexpectedly found a relationship between school achievement and delinquency and that his original hypothesis was not supported.
   d. Collect new data that support his original hypothesis.

5. A researcher is collecting information on juvenile and adult arrest records as a part of a large study on criminal careers. She promises the subjects that no identifying information will be publicly disclosed. She has assured subjects of their

    a. anonymity
    b. confidentiality
    c. informed consent
    d. legal liability

6. Dr. Cudney distributes questionnaires at a mall and asks the subjects not to put their name on the paper. Subjects are asked to drop the completed questionnaires in a locked box when they are finished filling out their responses. This researcher can reasonably assure these subjects of their

    a. anonymity
    b. confidentiality
    c. informed consent
    d. anonymity and confidentiality

7. College seniors taking a final exam encounter a short questionnaire at the end of their test. Without further information to indicate otherwise, the students assume it is part of their exam. All students complete the questionnaire. The professor who administered this exam/questionnaire failed to consider which of the following ethical issues? (You may choose more than one response.)

    a. deception
    b. voluntary participation
    c. confidentiality
    d. all of the above

8. Which one of the following statements characterizes the purpose of institutional review boards (IRB)?

    a. criminally prosecute unethical researchers
    b. make decisions regarding the units of analysis in the study
    c. determine whether a study assures the anonymity of subjects
    d. determine whether a study minimizes the potential for harm to subjects

9. Which of the following procedures are recommended by IRB guidelines to deal with prisoners as research subjects? (You may choose more than one response.)

    a. random selection of subjects
    b. adequate reward for participation, such as added privileges for participants
    c. at least one member of the IRB must be designated to represent the interests of prisoners
    d. anonymity of the research subjects

10. No harm to participants is an important ethical issue in research. This includes which of the following? (You may choose more than one response.)

    a. protecting the researcher from legal prosecution
    b. minimizing embarrassment of subjects
    c. protecting the researcher from physical harm
    d. minimizing emotional harm inflicted upon the subjects

11. Which one of the following is an example of deception?

    a. A field researcher studying gang behavior spends time hanging out on the street talking with gang members. He does not tell the gang members that he is a researcher.
    b. Subjects in a study of domestic violence are given a questionnaire and told that it concerns issues related to "family life".
    c. Both a and b are examples of deception.
    d. Both examples are justified, and would not be considered examples of deception.

12. Informed consent is typically used to satisfy

    a. confidentiality
    b. voluntary participation
    c. anonymity
    d. deception of subjects

13. A researcher is testing out a new behavior modification program for prison inmates, in which attitudinal change and prosocial behavior are rewarded with time spent outside the prison walls. The most ethical way to assign prisoners to either the experimental group, or control group in this study is

    a. through random selection.
    b. to ask for volunteers.
    c. to assign all prisoners to the experimental group.
    d. assign those prisoners with the longest time spent behind bars to the experimental group.

14. The Tearoom Trade study described in the text has been criticized with failing to justify which of the following ethical issues? (You may choose more than one response.)

   a.   informed consent
   b.   confidentiality
   c.   deception
   d.   nonrandom assignment

15. The prison simulation study described in the text attempted to protect subjects from harm by

   a.   having ongoing counseling sessions with subjects over the course of the study.
   b.   screening potential participants for physical or psychological problems at the beginning of the study.
   c.   allowing all subjects to go home and return to the simulated prison during the course of the study.
   d.   paying subjects to participate.

True/False Questions

1.   Because ethical considerations represent a compromise in criminal justice research, coupled with the fact that they are somewhat subtle and less obvious, most researchers believe that they are of secondary importance.

   a.   true
   b.   false

2.   The problem in criminal justice research--and probably in life--is that ethical considerations are not always apparent to us.

   a.   true
   b.   false

3.   Balancing the potential benefits from doing research against the possibility of harm to the people being studied--or harm to others--is a fundamental ethical dilemma in all research.

   a.   true
   b.   false

4. If researchers are concerned about ethical considerations associated with a particular form of data collection, researchers are wise to collect data through interviews, if possible, since subjects will not be harmed through this method.

   a. true
   b. false

5. As a general principle, possible harm to subjects may be justified if the potential benefits of the study outweigh the harm the study might cause.

   a. true
   b. false

6. A major tenant of medical and social science research ethics is that experimental participation must be randomly allocated.

   a. true
   b. false

7. A survey respondent or other person being studied may be considered anonymous when the researcher cannot identify a given piece of information with a given person.

   a. true
   b. false

8. Information provided by a study respondent is considered confidential when the researcher cannot identify the information provided by the specific respondent.

   a. true
   b. false

9. It is always wrong and unethical to deceive people about your identity as a researcher.

   a. true
   b. false

10. The norm of voluntary participation is usually satisfied by informing subjects about research procedures, then obtaining their consent to participate.

    a. true
    b. false

Essay Questions

1.   The text mentions that juveniles and prisoners are two groups that require special ethical protections. Review this discussion in the text and explain why these special protections are required.

2.   Consider the Kansas City Preventive Patrol Experiment. Identify a potential ethical problem that could be levied against this experiment. Next, provide two reasons why this experiment should be conducted, and be sure to defend your positions from an ethical standpoint.

Chapter 9

Overview of Data Collection and Sampling

I. *Introduction*

    A.   We have two purposes in this chapter: first to call your attention to some general issues in actual data collection, and second to discuss ❿ ❿ ❿

    B.   As is the case with most aspects of designing and executing criminal justice research, the choices you make about data collection and sampling depend on ❿ ❿ ❿

    C.   Sampling is the process of selecting observations: Sampling is ordinarily used to select observations for one of two related reasons.

        1.   First, it is often not possible to collect information from all persons or other units you wish to study.

        2.   The second reason for sampling observations is that it is often not necessary to collect data from ❿ ❿ ❿

II. *Three Sources of Data*

    ◇   We could measure crime by asking people questions about victimization or about offenses they have committed, by observing actual behavior, or by using some source of existing data; that is, asking questions, ❿ ❿ ❿

III. *Asking Questions*

    A.   In criminal justice and other types of social science research, when we collect data by asking people questions we often employ some form of survey method. (e.g., The National Crime Victimization Survey (NCVS) and the Monitoring the Future Survey).

        1.   A formal questionnaire that embodies operationalizations of concepts is a key element in these and other surveys.

        2.   The survey method is flexible and one of the most common approaches to gathering data in criminal justice <u>and other social science</u> research.

B.   Sometimes small groups of subjects are brought together for structured discussion of some research question. Referred to as focus groups, this technique was developed as a market research tool to explore how targeted consumers might respond to some new product or advertising campaign being considered (Krueger, 1994).

    1.   Groups of 12 to 15 subjects are selected according to some criteria, and engaged in ❍ ❍ ❍

    2.   Focus groups are increasingly used in criminal justice research.

IV.   *Making Observations*

   A.   Direct observation encompasses a broad range of methods for gathering data, from counting the number of participants who attend a community crime prevention meeting to urinalysis tests for drug use.

    1.   The defining characteristic of direct observation is obtaining measurements by observing behavior, traces of behavior, or physical objects without interacting with research subjects.

    2.   Direct observation does ❍ ❍ ❍

   B.   Forms of direct observation other than conducting laboratory tests of drug use present other types of problems.

V.   *Examining Written Records*

   A.   Many measurements are made by consulting written documents or other types of records.

    1.   Rather than directly observing criminal behavior, or asking subjects about arrests or convictions, researchers commonly examine records maintained by public agencies as sources for measures of something like criminal history.

    2.   As is the case with other ways of collecting data, written records are used in a variety of ways, corresponding roughly ❍ ❍ ❍

    3.   Criminal justice researchers frequently make use of information routinely collected by government agencies and made available to the general public.

    4.   Virtually all public agencies maintain other types of records for their own use that are not normally released to the general public but that may be ❍ ❍ ❍

B. Court decisions form another type of written record that is fundamental to conducting legal research.

    1. Judicial opinions express principles of law that attorneys and legal scholars regularly consult.

    2. Analyzing court decisions is a specialized example of content analysis, where information from documents, normally text, is systematically examined by researchers.

C. That data from written records which were originally collected either through observation or by asking people questions raises an important issue: if you will use data from written records in your research, it is essential that you understand how those data were originally collected.

VI. *Sources of Data Compared*

    ◇ As you design a research or evaluation project, you will have to consider choices about ❂ ❂ ❂ .

    1. Such choices are ultimately linked to your purposes in conducting research, subject to constraints on what is possible and, ❂ ❂ ❂ .

    2. You may find that multiple measures of some concept are needed.

VII. *Measurement Validity and Reliability*

A. Of course, in making plans for data collection, you'll be attentive to ❂ ❂ ❂ .

    ◇ When you begin to think more specifically about actually making measurements and when you actually begin collecting data, you often gain insights into validity and reliability questions that you might have overlooked in the design stage.

B. In making decisions about measurement and data collection, be prepared to ❂ ❂ ❂ in case you encounter some unexpected difficulty or ambiguity.

    1. After you begin to make actual observations, deficiencies may become evident in what ❂ ❂ ❂ .

    2. More commonly, collecting data will reveal potential reliability problems that are difficult to anticipate in the design stages of a research project.

    3. Unless you are using measures and data-collecting techniques that have been widely adopted and accepted by others, you are well advised to continually evaluate measurement and data-collection procedures.

VIII.   *Obtrusive and Unobtrusive Measures*

    A.   A distinction is often made between obtrusive and ◑ ◑ ◑   .

         1.   In obtrusive or reactive measurement, research subjects ◑ ◑ ◑   .

         2.   Unobtrusive measurement does not involve direct interaction between researchers and subjects, and the latter are not aware that they are being studied.

    B.   Unobtrusive measures are often preferred because the possibility of validity threats due to ◑ ◑ ◑   .

    C.   You should, however, carefully consider what kinds of measurement are obtrusive and unobtrusive.

    D.   Rather than describe measures as obtrusive or unobtrusive, it is more accurate to consider the extent to which the measurement process involves direct interaction with research subjects.

         1.   Rather than distinguish between obtrusive and unobtrusive measurement, it is more useful to focus on reducing bias or threats to validity in the measurement process more generally.

         2.   If you suspect that interactive data collection such as a survey will produce biased measures, you should try to develop some noninteractive measures or other procedures that will reduce the potential bias.

IX.   *Be Careful, But Be Creative*

    A.   We urge you to be cautious in formulating questionnaire items, making direct observations, or using data that ◑ ◑ ◑   .

         1.   Being attentive to questions of validity and reliability are critical first steps to careful measurement and data collection.

         2.   If you use written records, learn ◑ ◑ ◑   .

    B.   Being careful is important, but so is being creative.

X.   *The Logic of Probability Sampling*

    A.   If all members of a population were identical in all respects--all demographic characteristics, attitudes, experiences, behaviors, and so on--there would be no need for careful sampling procedures.

1. In such a case, any sample would indeed be sufficient.
2. In this extreme case of homogeneity, in fact, one case would be sufficient as a sample to study characteristics of the whole population.

B. When we speak of "bias" in connection with sampling, this simply means those selected are not "typical" or "representative" of the larger populations they have been chosen from.

XI. *Representativeness and Probability of Selection*

A. Representativeness—A sample will be representative of the population from which it is selected if the aggregate characteristics of the sample closely approximate those ◉ ◉ ◉

   ✧ <u>Notice that</u> samples need not be representative in all respects; representativeness is limited to characteristics that are relevant to the substantive interests of the study.

B. A basic principle of probability sampling is that a sample will be representative of the population from which it is selected if all members of the population ◉ ◉ ◉

C. Probability sampling offers two special advantages.

1. First, probability samples, although never perfectly representative, are typically more representative than other types of samples because the biases discussed in the preceding section are avoided.
2. Second, and more important, probability theory ◉ ◉ ◉

XII. *Sampling Concepts and Terminology*

A. **Element**—An *element* is that unit about ◉ ◉ ◉

1. Typically, in survey research, elements are people or certain types of people.
2. However, other kinds of units can constitute the elements for criminal justice research: correctional facilities, gangs, <u>police beats</u>, or court cases might be the elements of a study.

B. **Population**— A *population* is the theoretically ◉ ◉ ◉

1. Although researchers must begin with careful specification of their population, poetic license usually permits them to phrase their reports in terms of the hypothetical universe.
2. The primary guide in this matter, as in most others, is that you should not mislead or deceive your readers.

C. **Study Population**—A *study population* is that aggregation of elements from which the ❍❍❍   .

    1. As a practical matter, you are seldom in a position to guarantee that every element meeting the theoretical definitions laid down actually has a chance of being selected in the sample.
    2. Often researchers decide to limit their study populations.

D. **Sampling Unit**—*A sampling unit* is that element or set of elements considered for selection in ❍❍❍   .

    1. In the simplest case, termed a *single-stage sample*, the sampling units are the same as the elements.

    2. However, in more complex research designs the terms *primary sampling units*, *secondary sampling units*, and *final sampling units* are used to designate successive stages of research.

E. **Sampling Frame**—A **sampling frame** is the actual list of sampling units from which the sample, or some stage of the sample, is selected.

    1. In single-stage sampling designs, the sampling frame is simply a ❍❍❍

    2. In practice, existing sampling frames often define the study population rather than the other way around.

F. **Observation Unit**—An *observation unit*, or unit of data collection, is an element or aggregation of elements from which information is collected.

    1. Again, the unit of analysis and unit of observation are often the same, but that need not be the case.
    2. Thus, the researcher may interview heads of households (the observation units) to collect information about all members of the household (the units of analysis).

G. **Variable**—A **variable** is a set of ❍❍❍   :
    gender, age, employment status, and so forth.

132

1. The elements of a given population may be described in terms of their individual attributes on a given variable.
2. A variable, by definition, must possess variation -- it must vary.

H. **Parameter**—A *parameter* is the ❂ ❂ ❂   .

1. An important portion of criminal justice research involves the estimation of population parameters on the basis of sample observations.

I. **Statistic**—A *statistic* is the summary description of a given variable in a sample.

◇ Sample statistics are used to make ❂ ❂ ❂   .

J. **Sampling Error**—Probability sampling methods seldom, if ever, provide statistics exactly equal to the parameters that they are used to estimate.

◇ Probability theory, however, permits us to estimate the degree of error to be expected for a given sample design.

K. **Confidence Levels and Confidence Intervals**—We express the accuracy of our sample statistics in terms of a level of confidence that the statistics fall within a specified interval from the parameter.

◇ As the confidence interval is expanded for a given statistic, our confidence increases.

XIII. *Probability Sampling Theory*

A. The ultimate purpose of sampling is to select a set of elements from a population in such a way that descriptions of those elements (statistics) accurately portray the parameters of the total population from which the elements are selected.

1. Probability sampling enhances the likelihood of accomplishing this aim and also provides methods for estimating ❂ ❂ ❂   .

2. *Random selection*—Each element has an equal chance of selection independent of any other event in the selection process.

B. The reasons for using random selection methods are two fold.

1. First, this procedure serves as a check on conscious or unconscious bias on the part of the researcher.

2. More important, random selection offers access to the body of probability theory, which provides the basis for estimates of population parameters and estimates of error.

XIV. *The Sampling Distribution of Ten Cases*

✧ The progression of sampling distributions is clear. Every increase in sample size improves the distribution of estimates of the mean <u>in two related ways</u>.

1. First, in the distribution for samples of five for example, there are no sample means at the extreme ends of the distribution.
2. The second way sampling distributions improve with larger samples is that sample means ◐ ◑ ◐ .

XV. *Binomial Sampling Distribution*

A. If many independent random samples are selected from a population, the sample statistics provided by those samples will be distributed around the population parameter in a known way.

1. Probability theory gives us a formula for estimating how closely the sample statistics are clustered around the true value.
2. This formula contains three factors: the parameter, the sample size, and the standard error (a measure of sampling error):

$$s = \sqrt{\frac{P \times Q}{n}}$$

3. Symbols: P, Q = the population parameters for the binomial;
n = number of cases in each sample;
s = standard error

B. In probability theory, the standard error is a valuable piece of information, because it indicates the extent to which the sample estimates will be distributed around the population parameter.

1. Specifically, probability theory indicates that certain proportions of the sample estimates will fall within specified increments--each equal to one standard error--from ◐ ◑ ◐ .
2. Approximately 34 percent (.3413) of the sample estimates will fall within one standard error increment above the population parameter, and another 34 percent will fall within one standard error increment below the parameter.

3. We know that roughly two-thirds (68 percent) of the samples will give estimates <u>between 45 and 55 percent, which is</u> within 5 percent of the parameter,which in a binomial distribution is 50 percent, or the exact point where there is no difference between P and Q.

4. The standard error is also a function of the sample size--an inverse function. As the sample size increases, the standard error decreases.

C. Whereas probability theory specifies that 68 percent of that fictitious large number of samples would produce estimates falling within one standard error of the parameter, we turn the logic around and infer that any single random sample has a 68 percent chance of falling within that range.

1. We are 68 percent confident that our sample estimate is within one standard error of the ❂ ❂ ❂ .

2. We are 95 percent confident that the sample statistic is within two standard errors of the parameter, and so forth.

3. We are virtually positive (99.9 percent) that we are within three standard errors of the true value.

D. However, we have already noted that we seldom ❂ ❂ ❂

1. To resolve this dilemma, we substitute our sample estimate for the parameter in the formula; lacking the true value, we substitute the best available guess.

2. The result of these inferences and estimations is that we are able to estimate a population parameter and also the expected degree of error on the basis of one sample drawn from a population.

E. The logic of confidence levels and confidence intervals also provides the basis for determining the ❂ ❂ ❂ .

1. Once you have decided on the degree of sampling error you can tolerate, you will be able to calculate the number of cases needed in your sample.

XVI. *Populations and Sampling Frames*

✧ Although it is necessary for the research consumer, student, and researcher to understand the theoretical foundations of sampling, it is no less important that they appreciate the less-than-perfect conditions that exist in the field.

1. The present section is devoted to a discussion of one aspect of field conditions that requires a compromise with regard to theoretical conditions and assumptions.

2. A sampling frame is the list or quasi-list of elements from which a probability sample is selected.

3. Properly drawn samples provide information appropriate for describing the population of elements composing the sampling frame-nothing more.

4. Studies of organizations are often the simplest from a sampling standpoint because organizations typically have membership lists.

5. Other lists of individuals may be especially relevant to the research needs of a particular study.

6. Telephone directories are frequently used for "quick-and-dirty" public opinion polls.

XVII. Types of Sampling Designs

◇ Up to this point, we have focused on simple random sampling. However, you have a number of options in choosing your sampling method, and you will seldom if ever choose simple random sampling.

1. First, with all but the simplest sampling frame, simple random sampling is not feasible.

2. Second, simple random sampling may ❂ ❂ ❂

XVIII. Simple Random Sampling

◇ As noted **simple random sampling** is the basic sampling method assumed in the statistical computations of social research.

1. Once a sampling frame has been established in keeping with the guidelines we've presented, to use simple random sampling the researcher assigns a single number to each element in the list, not skipping any number in the process.

2. A table of random numbers, or a computer program for generating them, is then used to select elements for the sample.

XIX. Systematic Sampling

A. In systematic sampling, elements in the total list are chosen (systematically) for inclusion in the sample.

1. If the list contains 10,000 elements and you want a sample of 1,000, you select every tenth element for your sample.

2. To ensure against any possible human bias in using this method, you should select the first element at random.

3.   This method is technically referred to as a systematic sample ◐ ◐ ◐ .

B.   There is one danger involved in systematic sampling.

      1.   The arrangement of elements in the list can make systematic sampling unwise.

      2.   In considering a systematic sample from a list, then, you should carefully examine the nature of that list. If the elements are arranged in any particular order, you should figure out whether that order will bias the sample to be selected and take steps to counteract any possible bias.

      3.   In summary, however, systematic sampling is usually superior to simple random sampling, in convenience if nothing else.

XX.   *Stratified Sampling*

A.   **Stratification** sampling is not an alternative to random and systematic methods, but it represents a ◐ ◐ ◐ .

      ◇   Stratified sampling is a method for obtaining a greater degree of representativeness--decreasing the probable sampling error.

B.   Rather than selecting your sample from the total population at large stratified sampling procedures attempt to ensure that appropriate numbers of elements are drawn from homogeneous subsets of that population.

      1.   Even more complex stratification methods are possible.

      2.   The ultimate function of stratification, then, is to organize the population into homogeneous subsets (with heterogeneity between subsets) and to select the appropriate number of elements from each.

      3.   The choice of stratification variables typically depends on ◐ ◐ ◐ .

      4.   In selecting stratification variables from among those available, however, you should be concerned primarily with those that are presumably related to variables that you want to represent accurately.

      5.   Stratified sampling ensures the proper representation of the stratification variables to ◐ ◐ ◐ .

XXI.   *Disproportionate Stratified Sampling*

A.   Another use of stratification is to purposively produce samples that are not representative of a population on some variable.

B.   Disproportionate stratification is a way of obtaining sufficient numbers of "rare" cases by ◐ ◐ ◐ .

1.   The best example of disproportionate sampling in criminal justice is a national crime survey, where one goal is to obtain some minimum number of crime victims in a sample.
2.   The British Crime Survey (BCS), for instance, is a nationwide survey of people aged 16 and over in England and Wales. Conducted <u>approximately every other year</u> since 1982, the ❍ ❍ ❍

XXII. *Multistage Cluster Sampling*

A.   Situations when sampling procedures are considered ideal occur when straightforward selection of population elements are included for study from existing lists.

   ✧   Unfortunately, however, many interesting research problems require the selection of samples from populations that cannot be easily listed for sampling purposes.

B.   **Cluster sampling**—May be used when it is either impossible or impractical to ❍ ❍ ❍

   1.   It is often the case, however, that the population elements are already grouped into subpopulations, and a list of those subpopulations either exists or can be created.
   2.   Multistage cluster sampling, then, involves the repetition of two basic steps: listing and sampling.
   3.   The list of primary sampling units (city blocks) is compiled and, perhaps stratified for sampling.
   4.   Then a sample of those units is selected. The list of secondary sampling units is then sampled, and so forth
   5.   Cluster sampling is highly recommended by its efficiency, but the price of that efficiency is ❍ ❍ ❍
   6.   A good general guideline for cluster design is to maximize the number of clusters selected while decreasing the number of elements within each cluster.

XXIII. *Multistage Cluster Sampling with Stratification*

A.   Thus far, we have looked at cluster sampling as though a simple random sample were selected at each stage of the design. In fact, stratification techniques can be used to ❍ ❍ ❍

B.   Once the primary sampling units (e.g., law enforcement agencies) have been grouped according to the relevant, available stratification variables, either simple random or systematic sampling techniques can be used to select the sample.

1.   You might select a specified number of units from each group or stratum, or you might arrange the stratified clusters in a continuous list and systematically sample that list.
2.   There is no reason why stratification could not take place at each level of sampling.

XXIV. *Illustration: Two National Crime Surveys*

✧   In this regard, the different components of sampling can be tailored to specific purposes in much the same way research design principles can be modified to suit various needs.

1.   Since sample frames suitable for simple random sampling are often not available, multistage cluster sampling is used to ❶ ❷ ❸

2.   Stratification can be added to ensure that samples are representative of important variables. And samples may be designed to produce elements that are ❶ ❷ ❸   .

XXV. *National Crime Victimization Survey*

A.   Although various parts of the NCVS have been modified since the surveys were begun in 1972, basic sampling strategies have remained relatively unchanged.

✧   The survey seeks to represent the nationwide population of persons aged 12 and over who are living in households.

B.   Since there is no national list of households <u>in the U.S.</u>, multistage sampling must be used to get from larger units to households and their residents.

1.   The national sampling frame used in the first stage defines primary sampling units (PSUs) as either large metropolitan areas, nonmetropolitan counties, or a group of contiguous counties (to represent rural areas.)
2.   The largest PSUs are specified as "self-representing" and are automatically included in the first stage of sampling. The remaining PSUs are then stratified by size, population density, reported crimes, and other variables into about 150 strata.
3.   Subsequent stages first select census enumeration districts (defined in each decennial census) through systematic sampling, again with a probability proportionate to size.

4.   Next, clusters of approximately four housing units are selected from each enumeration district.

5.   For the 1994 NCVS, these procedures yielded a sample of approximately <u>56,000</u> housing units. Completed interviews were obtained from about <u>120,000</u> household occupants.

XXVI. *British Crime Survey*

A.   Fundamental changes in sampling procedures were introduced in the 1992 BCS, and remain essentially similar for the most current survey.

1.   While NCVS respondents are interviewed every six months to provide annual estimates of victimization, the BCS has been ❍ ❍ ❍

2.   While NCVS sampling procedures began with demographic units and worked down to selecting housing unit, the BCS began with electoral districts and eventually selected households that were recorded on lists of <u>addresses organized by post office codes, similar to U.S. zip codes.</u>

B.   The first stage of sampling for the 1992 BCS drew 289 Parliamentary constituencies, or districts from which members of the House of Commons are elected.

1.   Parliamentary constituencies were stratified by ❍ ❍ ❍

2.   Within constituencies, two sample points were then selected from a listing of postal code prefixes.

3.   Stage 3 involved dividing each sample point into four segments with approximately equal numbers of mail delivery addresses.

4.   One of these four segments was selected at random, and a starting point for systematic sampling was then randomly selected.

5.   Each segment yielded about 29 addresses for inner city areas, and 25 addresses for areas outside inner cities.

6.   As mentioned earlier, this oversample was done to produce a larger number of crime victims than might be obtained through strictly proportionate sampling procedures, such as those used in the NCVS.

7.   Household residents aged 16 and over were listed, and one randomly selected by interviewers.

C.   The NCVS uses *proportionate* sampling to select a large number of respondents who may then represent the relatively rare attribute of victimization.

D.   The BCS sampled a *disproportionate* number of inner-city respondents, more likely to be victims of crime, and was able to ❍ ❍ ❍

XXVII.   Probability Sampling in Review

◇   Depending on the field situation, probability sampling can be very simple, or it can be extremely difficult, time consuming, and expensive. Whatever the situation, however, it is usually the preferred method for selecting study elements.

1.   First, probability sampling avoids ❂ ❂ ❂

2.   Second, probability sampling permits estimates of sampling error.

3.   In spite of the preceding comments, it is sometimes not possible to use standard probability sampling methods.

XXVIII.   Nonprobability Sampling

A.   You can no doubt envision situations in which it would be either impossible or unfeasible to select the kinds of probability samples we have described.

B.   Moreover, as we'll see, there are times when probability sampling wouldn't be appropriate if possible. In many such situations, nonprobability sampling procedures are called for.

XXIX.   Purposive or Judgmental Sampling

A.   Occasionally it may be appropriate to select a sample on the basis of your own knowledge of the population, its elements, and the nature of your research aims--in short, based on ❂ ❂ ❂

B.   In some instances, you may wish to study a small subset of a larger population in which many members of the subset are easily identified, but the enumeration of all of them would be nearly impossible.

1.   Criminal justice research often focuses on comparisons of practices in different jurisdictions--cities or states, for example.

2.   Purposive or judgmental sampling may also be used to ❂ ❂ ❂

3.   Pretesting a questionnaire is another situation where purposive sampling is common.

XXX.   Quota Sampling

A.   Like probability sampling, quota sampling addresses the issue of representativeness, though the two methods approach the issue quite differently.

1.   Quota sampling begins with a matrix describing the characteristics of the target population you wish to represent.

2.   Once such a matrix has been created and a relative proportion assigned to each cell in the matrix, you collect data from ◐ ◐ ◐

3.   All the persons in a given cell are then assigned a weight appropriate to their portion of the total population.

B.   Quota sampling has some inherent problems.

1.   First, the quota frame (the proportions that different cells represent) must be accurate, and it is often difficult to get ◐ ◐ ◐

2.   Second, biases may exist in the selection of sample elements within a given cell--even though its proportion of the population is accurately estimated.

3.   On the other hand, quota and purposive sampling may be combined to produce samples that are intuitively, if not statistically, representative.

XXXI. Reliance on Available Subjects

◇   Relying on available subject-that is, stopping people at a street corner or some other location--is sometimes referred to as convenience sampling.

1.   However, it seldom produces data of any general value.
2.   Reliance on available subjects can be an appropriate sampling method in some applications. In general, however, it is justified only if the researcher wants to study the characteristics of people passing the sampling point at some specified time.
3.   If you can safely assume that no systematic pattern generates elements of a process, then a sample of available elements as they happen to pass by can be considered to be representative.

XXXII. Snowball Sampling

A.   Most commonly used in field observation studies or specialized interviewing, snowball samples begin by identifying a single or small number of subjects, then ◐ ◐ ◐

1.   Criminal justice research on active criminals or deviants frequently employs snowball sampling techniques.
2.   Initial contact is often made by consulting criminal justice agency records to identify, say, someone convicted of <u>auto theft</u> and placed on probation. That person would be interviewed and asked to ◐ ◐ ◐

B.   Snowball samples are essentially variations on purposive samples (e.g., you want to sample juvenile gangs members) and on samples of available subjects (sample elements identify other sample elements for you).

   1.   And like other types of nonprobability samples, snowball samples are most appropriate when it is ❂ ❂ ❂

   2.   Furthermore, snowball techniques may be necessary when the target population is difficult to locate or even identify.

Key Words and Terms

EPSEM samples	obtrusive and unobtrusive measures
probability sampling	element
population	study population
sampling unit	sampling frame
observation unit	variable
parameter	statistic
sampling error	confidence levels and confidence intervals
simple random sampling	systematic sampling
stratified sampling	disproportionate stratified sampling
multistage cluster sampling	purposive or judgmental sampling
quota sampling	snowball sampling

Multiple Choice Questions

1.   You would like to study the commission of crimes in a shopping mall parking lot. You have decided that you will collect data by walking around the perimeter of the parking lot, to discover actions of the people who enter and leave the lot. Which type of data source would this represent.

   a.   asking questions.
   b.   making observations.
   c.   examining written records.
   d.   none of the above.

2.	The State of California is interested in finding out how lawyers in Los Angeles feel about determinant sentencing laws and its impact on fairness in sentencing. The researcher in charge goes to the county courthouse in Los Angeles, stands outside the door of the office of the clerk of the court, and interviews all lawyers leaving the office who are wearing red ties. A sample of 250 lawyers is gathered through the use of this method. Which error, if any, has been committed by using this method?

	a.	unobtrusiveness.
	b.	conscious bias.
	c.	unconscious bias.
	d.	racial bias.

3.	Probability sampling methods allow a researcher to

	a.	confidently estimate the amount of sampling error that should be expected in a given sample.
	b.	draw a sample whose characteristics are representative of the population from which it was selected.
	c.	give every member of a population some known nonzero probability of being selected into the sample.
	d.	all of the above are true of probability sampling methods.

4.	The unit about which information is collected and that provides the basis of analysis is known as

	a.	a population.
	b.	a sampling frame.
	c.	an observation unit.
	d.	an element.

5.	The actual list of sampling units from which the sample, or some stage of the sample, is selected is known as a

	a.	sampling frame.
	b.	parameter.
	c.	study population.
	d.	population.

6.   A researcher is studying attitudes of the public about fear of child abduction. She has decided that she will telephone, at random, potential interviewees. What is her sampling frame?

   a.   the telephone listings.
   b.   the operators.
   c.   the public.
   d.   none of these are her sampling frame.

7.   A sample is drawn using the following method. First, a list is made which consists of all of the undergraduates listed in the university directory. Then, every fifteenth name is chosen from the list to be included in the sample. This is an example of which type of sampling design?

   a.   simple random sampling.
   b.   systematic sampling.
   c.   stratified sampling.
   d.   multistage cluster sampling.

8.   The National Institute of Crime wishes to draw a representative sample of judges from across the country for a survey on judicial discretion in sentencing. The procedure is as follows: first, 15 states are chosen to be used in the sample. Then, a list of all judicial jurisdictions in each of the states is compiled. Then, from that list, a list of all judges within the chosen jurisdictions is made, and a sample is drawn. This is an example of which type of sampling design?

   a.   simple random sampling.
   b.   stratified sampling.
   c.   disproportionate stratified sampling.
   d.   multistage cluster sampling.

9.   You are attending an introductory college course in juvenile delinquency when everyone in the class is asked to complete a survey regarding attitudes toward media coverage of high profiles murder cases. This is an example of which type of sampling design.

   a.   convenience sampling.
   b.   simple random sampling.
   c.   multistage cluster sampling.
   d.   snowball sampling.

10. You are interested in studying gang activity in Los Angeles. You have managed to find a connection with a gang member who is willing to introduce you to other members of his gang. After interviewing these members, they introduce you to members of a related gang. This is an example of which type of sampling design?

    a. simple random sampling.
    b. quota sampling.
    c. snowball sampling.
    d. stratified sampling.

11. A criminal justice professor is interested in studying college student attitudes toward academic dishonesty. He administers a questionnaire to students in a large class he is teaching this semester. The sampling technique employed by this researcher is

    a. snowball sampling.
    b. systematic sampling.
    c. probability sampling.
    d. convenience sampling.

12. Simple random samples, systematic samples, stratified samples, and cluster samples are all examples of

    a. nonprobability samples.
    b. probability samples.
    c. sampling distributions.
    d. sampling frames.

13. A television news station wishes to explore citizen attitudes toward a political candidate. The researchers use a telephone directory and randomly select 300 people to interview. The people listed in the phone directory represent this study's

    a. sample size.
    b. population.
    c. sampling frame.
    d. sampling parameter.

14. A researcher is interested in examining fear of crime among college dorm residents. Her sample is drawn from a list of all the dorm rooms on one campus. She selects every 12th room on the list and calls these residents for an interview. This researcher has used which one of the following sampling designs?

    a.   simple random sampling
    b.   systematic sampling
    c.   quota sampling
    d.   stratified sampling

15. Dr. Dolmas wishes to examine home security measures taken by residents in a large city. He obtains a list of census tracts in the city, randomly selects a sample of these tracts, compiles a list of residences within each tract, and finally, randomly selects a sample of residences from each sampled tract. These residences represent the final sample to be studied. Dr. Dolmas has used which one of the following sampling techniques?

    a.   stratified sampling
    b.   quota sampling
    c.   multistage cluster sampling
    d.   disproportionate stratified sampling

True/False Questions

1. Dr. Hotaling has been awarded a grant to examine the frequency of graffiti on walls within the city where she lives. She will collect this data by observing buildings and other surfaces within the city and counting the number which had graffiti upon them. This would be an example of an unobtrusive measure.

    a.   true
    b.   false

2. A sample is representative of the population from which it is selected if the aggregate characteristics of the sample approximate those of the general population.

    a.   true
    b.   false

3. An EPSEM sample is one in which every member of a population has the same probability of being selected.

    a.   true
    b.   false

4.   A parameter is the summary description of a given variable in a population.

    a.   true
    b.   false

5.   Sample error may be reduced by increasing the size of the sample.

    a.   true
    b.   false

6.   Simple random sampling is the most commonly used form of sampling design.

    a.   true
    b.   false

7.   Simple random sampling would be a way to produce a sample which overrepresents a population on some particular variable, such as race.

    a.   true
    b.   false

8.   The sampling design used in the National Crime Victimization Survey is multistage cluster sampling.

    a.   true
    b.   false

9.   Nonprobability sampling is conducted in the same way as probability sampling, except with a smaller size.

    a.   true
    b.   false

10.   One strength of probability sampling is that such samples permit estimates of sampling error.

    a.   true
    b.   false

Essay Questions

1. What is the purpose of probability sampling theory? State the two major advantages that probability sampling gives researchers. How does random selection fit into the process?

2. Dr. Thomas has been awarded a grant in order to study teenage prostitution in Seattle. She knows only three teenage prostitutes in this area and needs to interview several more. What type of sampling design should she use? Why? Finally, what are some of the potential pitfalls of using the sampling design chosen?

3. The text discusses three sources of data: asking questions, making observations, and examining written records. Choose a criminal justice topic that interests you. Describe how you could use all three sources of measurement to answer different research questions related to your topic.

Chapter 10

Survey Research and Other Ways of Asking Questions

I.   *Introduction*

    A.   Survey research is a ❂ ❂ ❂   .

    B.   Survey research is perhaps the most frequently used mode of observation in <u>sociology and political science, and is often used in criminal justice research.</u>

II.   *Topics Appropriate to Survey Research*

    ✧   Surveys may be used for descriptive, ❂ ❂ ❂   .

        1.   They are chiefly used in studies that have individual people as the units of analysis.

        2.   However, this method can be used for other units of analysis, such as households or <u>organization,</u> but it is necessary that some individual persons act as respondents or informants.

III.   *Counting Crime*

    ✧   Asking people about victimizations is an alternative measure of crime that adjusts for some of the problems exhibited by data collected ❂ ❂ ❂   .

IV.   *Self Reports*

    A.   Robert O'Brien (1985:65) has described self-report surveys as "the dominant method in criminology for studying the ❂ ❂ ❂   ."

        ✧   For research topics that seek to explore or explain why people commit criminal, delinquent, or deviant acts, asking questions is currently the best available method.

    B.   Within the general category of self-report surveys, two different applications are distinguished by target population and ❂ ❂ ❂   .

        1.   Studies of offenders select samples of respondents known to have committed crimes, often prisoners. Typically the focus is on the frequency of <u>offending,</u> or how many crimes of various types are committed by active offenders over a period of time.

2. The other type of self-report survey focuses on the prevalence of <u>offending</u>, or how many people commit crimes, in contrast to the number of crimes committed by a target population of offenders. Such surveys typically employ samples that represent a broader population, such as U.S. households, adult males, or high school seniors.

C. Chapter 6 also mentioned some of the problems that emerge in self-report surveys, most notably validity and reliability.

1. General population surveys and surveys of offenders tend to present different types of difficulties.

2. Recall error and the reporting of fabricated offenses may be problems in a survey of high-rate offenders, (while respondents in general-population self-report surveys may be reluctant to disclose illegal behavior).

V. *Perceptions and Attitudes*

    ◇   <u>Another application of surveys in criminal justice is</u> to learn how ❂ ❂ ❂

1. Public views about sentencing policies, gun control, police performance, and drug abuse are often included in opinion polls.
2. Since the mid-1970s, a growing number of explanatory studies have been conducted on public perceptions about crime and crime problems.

VI. *Policy Proposals*

    ◇   The intractability of crime prompts a continual search for policy responses, a large number of which require participation, or at least approval by the general public.

VII. *Targeted Victim Surveys*

A. Victim surveys that target individual cities or neighborhoods are important tools for evaluating ❂ ❂ ❂

1. Many criminal justice programs seek to prevent or reduce crime in some specific area.
2. Although counts of crime before and after a policy change represent an obvious measure of program success, crimes reported to police cannot be used to evaluate many types of programs.

B. In general, surveys can be used to evaluate policy that seeks to change attitudes, beliefs, or other perceptions.

VIII. *Guidelines for Asking Questions*

    A.   Several general guidelines can assist you in framing and asking questions that serve as excellent operationalizations of variables.

    B.   You should also be aware of pitfalls that can result in useless and even misleading information.

IX. *Open-Ended and Closed-Ended Questions*

    A.   In asking questions, researchers have two <u>basic</u> options, <u>each of which can accommodate certain variations.</u>

        1.   We may ask *open-ended questions*, in which case the respondent is asked to ❍ ❍ ❍   .

        2.   In the other case -- *closed-ended questions* -- the respondent is asked to ❍ ❍ ❍   .

    B.   The chief shortcoming of closed-ended questions lies in the researcher's structuring of responses.

    C.   In the construction of closed-ended questions, you should be guided by two of the requirements for operationalizing variables stated in Chapter 5.

        1.   First, the response categories provided should be *exhaustive*: they should ❍ ❍ ❍   .

        2.   Second, the answer categories must be *mutually exclusive*: The respondent should not feel compelled to ❍ ❍ ❍   .

X. *Questions and Statements*

    A.   The term **questionnaire** suggests a collection of questions, but an examination of a typical questionnaire will probably reveal as many statements as questions.

    B.   Rensis Likert has greatly formalized this procedure through the creation of the Likert scale, a format in which respondents are asked to ❍ ❍ ❍   .

XI. *Make Items Clear*

    A.   It should go without saying that questionnaire items should be clear and unambiguous, but the broad proliferation of unclear and ambiguous questions in surveys makes the point worth stressing here.

B.   Frequently, researchers ask respondents for a single answer to a combination of questions. Such "double-barreled" questions are problematic and seem to occur most often when the researcher has personally identified with a complex question.

XII.   *Short Items are Best*

   ◇   In the interest of being unambiguous and precise and pointing to the relevance of an issue, the researcher is often led into long and complicated items. That should be avoided.

      1.   In the case of questionnaires respondents complete themselves, people are often unwilling to study an item in order to understand it.

      2.   The respondent should be able to read an item quickly, understand its intent, and ◉ ◉ ◉

      3.   In general , you should assume that respondents will read items quickly and give quick answers; therefore, you should provide clear, short items that will not be misinterpreted under those conditions.

XIII.   *Avoid Negative Items*

   ◇   The appearance of a negation in a questionnaire item ◉ ◉ ◉

XIV.   *Avoid Biased Items and Terms*

   ◇   The meaning of someone's response to a question depends in large part on the wording of the question asked. That is true of every question and answer.

      1.   Questions that encourage respondents to answer in a particular way are called ◉ ◉ ◉

      2.   The mere identification of an attitude or position with a prestigious person or agency can bias responses.

XV.   *General Questionnaire Format*

   ◇   The format of a questionnaire is just as important as the nature and wording of the questions asked. An improperly laid-out questionnaire can lead respondents to miss questions, can confuse them about the nature of the data desired, and in the extreme, may lead them to throw the questionnaire away.

      ◇   As a general rule, the questionnaire should be ◉ ◉ ◉

XVI.   *Contingency Questions*

    A.   Quite often in questionnaires, certain questions will be clearly relevant only to some of the respondents and irrelevant to others.

        1.   Frequently, this situation--realizing that the topic is relevant only to some respondents--will arise ❂ ❂ ❂

        2.   The subsequent questions in series such as these are called *contingency questions:* whether they are to be asked and answered is contingent on responses to the first question in the series.

    B.   There are several formats for contingency questions.

        1.   Such a question would apply to all respondents, and each would find an appropriate answer category.
        2.   Used properly, complex sets of contingency questions can even be constructed without confusing the respondent.

XVII.   *Matrix Questions*

    A.   Often, you will want to ask several questions that have the same set of answer categories.

        1.   This is typically the case whenever the Likert response categories are used.
        2.   In such cases it is often possible to construct a matrix of items and answers.

    B.   This format has a number of advantages.

        1.   First, it uses space ❂ ❂ ❂
        2.   Second, respondents will probably find it faster to complete a set of questions presented in this fashion.
        3.   In addition, this format may increase the comparability of responses given to different questions for the respondent as well as for the researcher.

    C.   There are some dangers inherent in using this format as well.

        1.   Its advantages may encourage you to structure an item so that the responses fit into the matrix format when a different, more idiosyncratic, set of responses might be more appropriate.
        2.   Also, the matrix question format can foster a response set among some respondents: they may develop a pattern of, say, ❂ ❂ ❂

3. Response sets can be reduced somewhat by alternating statements representing different orientations and by making all statements short and clear.

XVIII. *Ordering Questions in a Questionnaire*

A. The order in which questions are asked can also affect the answers given.

   1. First, the appearance of one question can affect the answers given to later ones.
   2. The safest solution is sensitivity to the problem. Although you cannot avoid the effect of question order, you should attempt to estimate what that effect will be.
   3. If the order of questions seems an especially important issue in a given study, you might ❾ ❾ ❾

B. The desired ordering of questions differs somewhat between self-administered questionnaires and interviews.

   1. It is usually best to begin a self-administered questionnaire with the ❾ ❾ ❾

   2. At the same time, however, the initial questions should be neither threatening nor sensitive.
   3. Requests for duller, demographic data (age, sex, and the like) should generally be placed at the end of a self-administered questionnaire.
   4. Just the opposite is generally true for in-person interview surveys.
   5. After a short introduction to the study, the interviewer can best begin by enumerating the members of the household, getting demographic data about each.
   6. Once the initial rapport has been established, the interviewer can then move into the area of ❾ ❾ ❾

XIX. *Self-Administered Questionnaires*

A. Although the mail survey is the typical method used in self-administered studies, several other common methods exist. In some cases, it may be appropriate to administer the questionnaire to a group of respondents gathered at the same place at the same time, such as police officers at roll call, or prison inmates at some specially arranged assembly.

B. Some recent experimentation has been conducted with regard to the home delivery of questionnaires.

1. A research worker delivers the questionnaire to the home of sample respondents and explains the study.
2. Then the questionnaire is left for the respondent to complete, and the researcher picks it up later.
3. Home delivery and the mail can be used ❍ ❍ ❍
4. In just the opposite method, questionnaires have been hand delivered by research office.

XX. Mail Distribution and Return

A. The basic method for data collection through the mail has been transmittal of a questionnaire, accompanied by a letter of explanation and a self-addressed, stamped envelope for returning the questionnaire.

   1. As a respondent, you are expected to complete the questionnaire, put it in the envelope, and return it.
   2. One big reason for not returning questionnaires is the complaint that ❍ ❍ ❍

B. Researchers have developed a number of ways to make the return of questionnaires easier.

   1. One development is a self-mailing questionnaire, requiring no return envelope. The questionnaire is designed so that when it is folded in a particular fashion, the return address appears on the outside.
   2. Anything you can do to make the job of completing and returning the questionnaire easier will improve your study.

C. One factor to consider in the actual mailing of questionnaires is timing.

   1. In most cases, the holiday months of ❍ ❍ ❍

   2. Overall mail volume is greatest during these periods, which can substantially slow down both distribution and return of questionnaires.

XXI. Warning Mailings, Cover Letters

A. The U.S. population, especially that proportion residing in urban areas, is becoming increasingly mobile. Certain types of warning mailings can also be somewhat effective in response rate.

   1. Warning mailings work like this. After generating a sample, a postcard is sent to the address of the selected respondent, with the notation "address correction requested" printed on the postcard.

2. In cases where someone has moved and not left a forwarding address, or more than one year has elapsed and the post office no longer has information about a new address, the postcard is returned marked something like "addressee unknown."

B. Selected persons who still reside at the original listed address are 'warned" in suitable language to expect a questionnaire in the mail. In such cases, postcards should ◉ ◉ ◉ .

C. Cover letters accompanying the actual questionnaire offer similar opportunities to increase response rates.

    1. First, the content of the letter is obviously important. Your message should communicate your reasons for conducting a survey, how and why the respondent was selected, and why it is important for the respondent to complete your questionnaire.

    2. The second aspect of cover letters is the ◉ ◉ ◉ .

D. Nevertheless, overall response rate is one guide to the representativeness of the sample respondents.

XXII. The Role of the Interviewer

◇ In-person interview surveys typically attain higher response rates than mail surveys. A properly designed and executed interview survey ought to achieve a completion rate of at least ◉ ◉ ◉ .

    1. The presence of an interviewer generally decreases the number of "don't knows" and "no answers."

    2. Interviewers can also provide a guard against ◉ ◉ ◉ .

    3. Finally, the interviewer can ◉ ◉ ◉ .

XXIII. Telephone Surveys

A. For years, telephone surveys had a bad reputation among professional researchers. Telephone surveys are limited by definition to ◉ ◉ ◉ .

    1. Over time, however, the telephone has become a standard fixture in almost all American homes.

    2. The Census Bureau estimates that 94 percent of all households now have telephones, so the earlier form of class bias has been substantially reduced.

    3. A related sampling problem involves unlisted numbers.

4.   This potential bias has been erased through a random-digit dialing (RDD), a technique that has advanced telephone sampling substantially.

B.   RDD samples use computer algorithms to generate lists of random telephone numbers -- usually the last four digits.

    1.   This procedure gets around the sampling problem of unlisted telephone numbers, but potentially creates an administrative problem instead.

    2.   Randomly generating telephone numbers produces numbers that are not in operation, or numbers that serve a business establishment or pay phone.

C.   Telephone surveys have many advantages that underlie the popularity of this method.

    1.   Probably the greatest advantages are money and time, in that order.

    2.   Interviewing by telephone, you can dress any way you please without affecting the answers respondents give.

    3.   Telephone surveys can give you greater control over data collection if several interviewers are engaged in the project.

    4.   A related advantage is rooted in the growing diversity of U.S. cities. Because many major cities have growing immigrant populations, interviews may need to be conducted in different languages.

    5.   Another important factor involved in the growing use of telephone surveys has to do with personal safety and concerns for the same.

D.   There are still problems involved in telephone interviewing.

    1.   The method is hampered by the proliferation of bogus "surveys," which are actually sales campaigns disguised as research.

    2.   Telemarketing is now easier and cheaper than ever. The volume of junk phone calls now rivals that of junk mail, and salespeople often begin their pitch by describing a "survey."

    3.   Residential phone customers have much greater control over incoming calls through the proliferation of answering machines and other new phone. services.

    4.   The ease with which people can hang up is, of course, another shortcoming of telephone surveys.

XXIV. *Computer-Assisted Interviewing*

A.   Much of the growth in telemarketing has been fueled by advances in computer and telecommunications technology.

    1.   Computers generate and dial phone numbers (in some cases computers even control recorded sales pitches).

2.   Beginning in the l980s, much of the same technology came to be widely used in telephone surveys, referred to as ◐ ◐ ◐
                                                                    (CATI).

3.   Interviewers wearing telephone headsets sit at computer workstations.

4.   Computer programs dial samples phone numbers, which can be either generated through random <u>digit dialing</u> or extracted from a database of phone numbers compiled from some source.

5.   As interviewers key in answers to each question, the computer program displays a new screen that presents the next question, until the end of the interview is reached.

B.   CATI systems offer several advantages over older procedures where an interviewer would work through a printed interview schedule.

1.   Speed is one obvious plus.

2.   CATI software immediately formats responses into a data file as they are keyed in, eliminating the ◐ ◐ ◐

C.   Accuracy is also enhanced by CATI systems in a couple of different ways.

1.   First CATI programs can be designed to accept only valid responses to any given questionnaire item.

2.   Second, the software can be programmed to automate contingency questions and skip sequences, thus ensuring that the interviewer skips over inappropriate items and rapidly gets to the next appropriate question.

XXV. Comparison of the Three Methods

A.   Self-administered questionnaires are generally ◐ ◐ ◐

1.   Moreover, if you use the self-administered mail format, it costs no more to conduct a national survey than a local one; the cost difference between a local and a national in-person interview survey would be much greater.

2.   Mail surveys typically require a small staff: one person can conduct a reasonable mail survey alone.

3.   Up to point, cost and speed are inversely related: in-person interview surveys can be completed very quickly if a large pool of interviewers is readily available and money is at hand to pay them.

B.   Self-administered surveys are usually more appropriate in dealing with ◐ ◐ ◐

C.   Interview surveys have many advantages, too.

            1.   For example, they are more appropriate where respondent literacy may be a problem.

            2.   Interview surveys also produce ◐ ◐ ◐

            3.   Interview surveys, moreover, have typically achieved higher completion rates than ◐ ◐ ◐

            4.   Although self-administered questionnaires may be more effective in dealing with sensitive issues, interview surveys are definitely more effective in dealing with complicated ones.

D.   Ultimately, you must balance all these advantages and disadvantages of the three methods in relation to: (1) your research needs and (2) ◐ ◐ ◐

XXVI. *Strengths and Weaknesses of Survey Research*

A.   Surveys are particularly useful in describing the characteristics of ◐ ◐ ◐

            1.   A carefully selected probability sample in combination with a standardized questionnaire offers the possibility of making refined descriptive statements about a neighborhood, a city, a nation, or some other large population.

            2.   Standardized questionnaires have an important strength in regard to measurement generally.

B.   At the same time, survey research has a number of weaknesses.

            1.   First, the requirement for standardization just mentioned might result in the fitting of round pegs into square holes.

            2.   Surveys often appear superficial in their coverage of ◐ ◐ ◐

            3.   Although surveys are flexible in the sense mentioned earlier, they are inflexible once interviewing has begun.

C.   Using surveys to study crime and criminal justice policy presents special challenges.

            ◇   Frequently the target population will include lower-income, transient persons who are difficult to contact through customary sampling methods.

D.   Survey research is generally weaker on validity and ◐ ◐ ◐

            1.   In comparison with field research, for instance, the artificiality of the survey format puts a strain on validity.

2.   Survey responses to many questions are, at best, approximate indicators of what we have in mind when we conceptualize fear of crime.

E.   Reliability is, in part, a different matter. Survey research, by presenting all subjects with a standardized stimulus, goes a long way toward eliminating unreliability in observations made by the researcher.

XXVII. Specialized Interviewing

A.   There is no precise definition of the term survey that enables us to distinguish a survey from other types of interview situations.

1.   As a rule of thumb, we can describe a sample survey (even one using nonprobability sampling methods) as an ❍ ❍ ❍ .

2.   In contrast, specialized interviewing focuses on the views and opinions only of those individuals who are interviewed.

B.   Quinn Patton (1990:280) distinguishes two variations of specialized interviews.

1.   The less structured alternative is to prepare a *general interview guide* that includes the issues, topics or questions you wish to cover. Issues are not presented to respondents in any standardized order.
2.   *The standardized open-ended interview* is more structured, using a series of specific questions arranged in a specified order.
3.   Questions are open-ended, but their format and presentation is standardized.

C.   Open-ended questions are ordinarily used because they better capture rich detail.

1.   The primary disadvantage of open-ended questions--having to categorize responses--is not a problem in specialized interviewing because of the small numbers of subjects, and because researchers are more interested in describing than generalizing.
2.   Case studies, where a researcher studies ❍ ❍ ❍ .

XXVIII. Focus Groups

A.   Surveys have two disadvantages in market research.

1.   First, a nationwide or large-scale probability survey can be ❍ ❍ ❍ .
2.   Second, it may be difficult to present advertising messages or other product images in a survey format.

B.   **Focus groups** have proven more suitable for many market research applications. In recent years, focus groups have been more widely used as substitutes for surveys in criminal justice and other social science research.

1.   In a focus group, typically ❂ ❂ ❂

2.   Although focus groups cannot be used to make statistical estimates about a population, members are nevertheless selected to represent a target population.

C.   Generalizations from focus groups to target populations cannot be precise, however a study by Ward and others (1991) found that focus-group and survey results can be quite consistent under certain conditions. They conclude that focus groups are most useful when

1.   precise generalization to a larger population is not necessary, and
2.   focus-groups participants and the larger population they are intended to represent are ❂ ❂ ❂

D.   Focus groups may also be used in combination with survey research in one of two ways.

1.   First, a focus group can be extremely valuable in ❂ ❂ ❂

2.   Second, after a survey has been completed and preliminary results tabulated, focus groups may be used to guide interpretation of some results.

E.   Focus groups are flexible and can be adapted to many uses in basic and applied research.

1.   Keep in mind, however, *Focus* means that researchers present specific questions or issues for direct discussion
2.   Group calls your attention to thinking about who will participate in the focused discussions. Like market researchers, you should select participants from a specific target population that relates to your research questions.

XXIX.   *Should You Do It Yourself?*

A.   The final issue we address in this chapter is who should conduct surveys.

1.   On the one hand, the different tasks involved in completing a survey require a lot of work and attention to detail.

162

2.   Consider the start-up costs involved in in-person or telephone interview surveys of any size. Finding, training, and paying interviewers is time consuming, not cheap, and requires some degree of expertise.

B.   If interview surveys are beyond your means, you might fall back on a mail survey.

1.   Few capital costs are involved. One or two persons can orchestrate a mail survey reasonably well at minimal expense.
2.   However, the business of completing a survey also involves a great deal of tedious work.
3.   So it's possible to do a mail survey yourself, but be prepared for lots of work; even then, it will be more work than you expect.

C.   Some methods are more or less appropriate than others for different kinds of research questions.

D.   The alternative to doing it yourself is to contract with ❂ ❂ ❂

Key Words and Terms

exhaustive	open-ended and closed-ended questions
mutually exclusive	questionnaire
contingency questions	matrix questions
general interview guide	self-administered questionnaires
standardized open-ended interview	telephone surveys
computer assisted interviewing	

Multiple Choice Questions

1.   Dr. Stevens found that only 30 percent of the questionnaires he mailed out to respondents were returned after a two-week period. A useful strategy to encourage more people to respond is

    a.   threatening letters
    b.   warning mailings
    c.   follow-up mailings
    d.   none of the above—30 percent is an acceptable response rate

2. Social desirability is one problem associated with self-report surveys regarding crime. Which of the following techniques would be useful in minimizing or avoiding this problem?

   a. use of a disclaimer.
   b. ask about other people's behavior first before asking about the respondent's behavior.
   c. use of euphemisms and less confrontational language when asking questions.
   d. all of the above are ways to avoid or minimize the problem.

3. A researcher is utilizing a technology that allows him to employ researchers who sit at workstations and use computer programs which dial phone numbers of prospective respondents in addition to guiding the interviewer through a series of questions to be asked. The technology is known as

   a. GSS.
   b. CATL.
   c. MATL.
   d. CATI.

4. A disadvantage of using focus groups is that it

   a. many influence the research outcome.
   b. may not combine easily with other research methods.
   c. may bias the researcher.
   d. may be expensive on a large scale.

5. A reason for contracting with a professional firm for a survey rather than conducting it yourself might be that

   a. drawing a sample is a complex process.
   b. they already have a pool of trained researchers.
   c. they are trained in the intricacies of questionnaire construction.
   d. all of the above.

6. Twenty-five percent of the sampled subjects in Dr. Leslie's in-person interview study refused to participate. This high refusal rate should prompt him to be concerned about

   a. response bias
   b. measurement reliability
   c. open-ended questions
   d. the neutrality of the interviewers

7.   Wearing a business suit is appropriate

    a.   in all interview situations
    b.   when interviewing people in prison
    c.   when interviewing high-level criminal justice officials
    d.   when interviewing mothers on welfare

8.   Which one of the following is not a strength of survey research?

    a.   Survey research makes large samples feasible.
    b.   Survey research is generally stronger on validity than observational research.
    c.   Surveys are useful in describing the characteristics of a large population.
    d.   Survey research is generally stronger on reliability than observational research.

9.   The following is an example of which type of question?

    Q1: How do you feel about drug legalization?

    a.   matrix question
    b.   contingency question
    c.   closed-ended question
    d.   open-ended question

10.   The following is an example of which type of question?

    2: What do you think will happen if marijuana is legalized?
        (a) drug use will increase
        (b) drug use will decrease
        (c) drug use will remain the same

    a.   matrix question
    b.   contingency question
    c.   closed-ended question
    d.   open-ended question

11. The following is an example of which type of question?

> Q3: Have you ever smoked marijuana?
> (a) yes
> (b) no --> if no answer Q4:
> Q4: Would the legalization of marijuana increase the likelihood that you will try it?
> (a) yes
> (b) no

    a.   matrix question
    b.   contingency question
    c.   two-stage question
    d.   conditional response question

12. Which of the following should be avoided when constructing a questionnaire? (You may choose more than one response.)

    a.   ambiguous questions
    b.   short items
    c.   contingency questions
    d.   placing the more interesting items toward the beginning

13. Which one of the following topics would be least appropriate to survey research?

    a.   counting the number of inmates in New York State prisons
    b.   attitudes toward the death penalty
    c.   citizen evaluation of a neighborhood watch program
    d.   behavior during a riot

14. Dr. Kuhns is interested in conducting a survey of prostitutes, many of whom are illiterate, in jail. Which one of the following survey methods would be most appropriate?

    a.   telephone interviews
    b.   in-person interviews
    c.   mail surveys
    d.   none of the above would be appropriate

15. Dr. Smith plans a case study of a serial killer on death row. Which one of the following survey methods would be most appropriate?

    a.   specialized interviewing
    b.   focus group
    c.   computer-assisted telephone interviewing
    d.   mail survey

True/False Questions

1. Criminal justice researchers are comforted by knowing that survey research is a very old technique, and many lessons have been learned with respect to using surveys efficiently for social science research.

   a. true
   b. false

2. Surveys may be used for descriptive, explanatory, exploratory, but not for applied research.

   a. true
   b. false

3. Asking people about victimizations is an alternative measure of crime that adjusts for some of the problems exhibited by data collected by police.

   a. true
   b. false

4. In general, surveys can be used to evaluate policy that seeks to change attitudes, beliefs, or other perceptions.

   a. true
   b. false

5. It is generally considered good form to study hard to discuss behaviors through surveys.

   a. true
   b. false

6. Rensis Likert has greatly formalized the form of questionnaires based on protocols used for constructing open-ended questions.

   a. true
   b. false

7. Double-barreled questions are those survey questions that could have two meanings, depending on how you interpret a specific word in question.

   a. true
   b. false

8. One strength of a well written matrix question is that this type of question will use space efficiently.

   a. true
   b. false

9. One strength of a well written matrix question is that this type of question can foster a response set.

   a. true
   b. false

10. The desired ordering of questions differs somewhat between self-administered questionnaires and interviews.

   a. true
   b. false

Essay Questions

1. Which of the following would be an appropriate topic for a survey in an evaluation study? Explain why each is appropriate or inappropriate.

   (a) The effect of community policing on increasing arrests for burglary.
   (b) The effects of community policing on citizen views of police effectiveness.

2. Discuss the use of the mail survey for self-administered questionnaires. What are some of the advantages and disadvantages of using the mail? How can response rate be increased when using mail surveys? Finally, describe a piece of research that provides a good example for the utility of self-administered mail survey.

3. Discuss the importance of monitoring returns of questionnaires. How can this activity help to identify possible biases in the sample? Illustrate your answer with a criminal justice example.

Chapter 11

FIELD RESEARCH

Chapter Outline

I. *Introduction*

    A.   Field research encompasses two different methods of obtaining data, direct observation and ● ● ●   .

        1.   Field research may yield qualitative data—observations not easily reduced to numbers—in addition to quantitative data.

        2.   For example, a field researcher studying burglars may note the number of times subjects had been arrested (quantitative), as well as whether individual burglars tended to select certain types of targets (qualitative).

    B.   Qualitative field research is often a theory--or ● ● ●

        1.   In many types of field studies, researchers do not have precisely defined ● ● ●   .

        2.   Field observation is often used to make sense out of an ongoing process that cannot be predicted in advance--making initial observations, developing tentative general conclusions that suggest particular types of further observations, making those observations and thereby revising your conclusions, and so forth.

        3.   Glaser and Straus (1967) refer to this process as ● ● ●   .

    C.   Field studies in criminal justice may also produce quantitative data that can be used to test hypotheses or ● ● ●   .

    D.   Compared to criminal justice professionals, researchers tend to be more concerned with generalizations and using systematic field research techniques to support generalizations.

        1.   In a sense, we all do field research whenever we observe or participate in social behavior and try to understand it.

        2.   Our focus here is on how to observe things in a systematic way that will be suitable for different research applications.

II.   *Topics Appropriate to Field Research*

   A.   One of the key strengths of field research is the ◐ ◐ ◐

      1.   This aspect of field research enhances its ◐ ◐ ◐   .
      2.   By going directly to the phenomenon under study and observing it as completely as possible, you can develop a deeper and fuller understanding of it.
      3.   This mode of observation, then, is especially, though not exclusively, appropriate to research topics that appear to defy simple quantification.
      4.   McCall (1978:8-9) states that observation is most appropriate for obtaining information about physical or social settings, behaviors, and events.

   B.   Field research is especially appropriate to the study of topics that can best be understood within ◐ ◐ ◐   .

      1.   For example, field research provides a superior method for studying how street-level drug dealers interpret behavioral and situational cues to distinguish potential customers, normal street traffic, and undercover police officers.
      2.   It would be difficult to study these skills through a survey.

III.   *The Various Roles of the Observer*

   A.   The term *field research* is broader and more inclusive than the frequently used term *participant observation*. Raymond Gold (1969:30-39) has discussed four different positions on a continuum of roles that field researchers may play in this regard ◐ ◐ ◐

      1.   Here we remind you of an ethical issue raised in Chapter 8. Is it ethical to deceive the people you are studying in the hope that they will confide in you as they will not confide in an identified researcher?
      2.   No researcher deceives his or her subjects solely for the purpose of deception. Rather, it is done in the belief that the data will be more valid and reliable, that the subjects will be more natural and honest if they do not know the researcher is doing a research project.

   B.   If the people being studied know they are being studied, they might ◐ ◐ ◐   .

      1.   First, they might ◐ ◐ ◐   .
      2.   Second, they might modify their speech and behavior to appear more respectable than would otherwise be the case.

3.   Third, the process being observed might be radically changed.
4.   On the other side of the coin, if you are a complete participant, you may affect what you are studying.
5.   Legal and physical risks present obstacles to the role of complete participant in field research among criminals or delinquents.
6.   Finally, complete participation in field studies of criminal justice institutions is ❶ ❷ ❸   .

C.   Because of these considerations—ethical, scientific, practical, and safety—the field researcher most often chooses a different role from that of complete participant. In Gold's terminology, you might choose the role of *participant-as-observer*.

1.   In this role, you would participate with the group under study, but you would make it clear that you were also undertaking research.
2.   There are dangers in this role also, however. The people being studied may shift much of their attention to the research project, and the process being observed may no longer be typical.
3.   Or, conversely, you may begin to "go native" and lose much of your ❶ ❷ ❸   .

D.   The *observer-as-participant* is one who identifies himself or herself as a researcher and interacts with the participants in the course of their routine activities but makes no pretense of actually being a participant.

1.   Researchers typically accompany police officers on patrol, for example, observing routine activities and the interactions between police and citizens.
2.   Spending several hours in the company of a police officer also affords opportunities for ❶ ❷ ❸   .

E.   The *complete observer*, at the other extreme, observes some location or process without becoming a part of it in any way.

1.   Quite possibly, the subjects of study might not realize they are being studied because of the researcher's unobtrusiveness.
2.   Although the complete observer is less likely to affect what is being studied and less likely to go native than the complete participant, he or she may be less able to develop a full appreciation of what is being studied.

F.   McCall (1978:45) points out an interesting and often unnoticed trade-off between whatever role the observer adopts and the observer's ability to learn from what she or he sees.

1.	Think carefully about the trade-off. It is most important that subjects not be affected by your role as observer, ❂ ❂ ❂

2.	More generally, the appropriate role for you as an observer hinges on what you want to learn and the opportunities and constraints that affect your field inquiry.

3.	Unfortunately, there are no clear guidelines for making this choice, and you must rely on your understanding of the situation and your own good judgment.

4.	In making your decision, however, you must be guided by both ❂ ❂ ❂

## IV.	*Asking Questions*

A.	Field research is often a matter of going where the action is and simply watching and listening. Sometimes it's appropriate to ask people questions and record their answers.

1.	Field research interviews are usually much less structured than those completed for surveys.

2.	Unstructured interviews are most appropriate when researchers have less knowledge about a topic, and in situations where it's more reasonable for researchers to have a casual conversation with a subject.

3.	Unstructured interviews are also appropriate when researchers and subjects are ❂ ❂ ❂

4.	In other field research situations, you should be prepared to conduct interviews that are somewhat more structured.

B.	On the other hand, one of the special strengths of field research is its flexibility in the field.

1.	You need to ask a question, hear the answer, interpret its meaning for your general inquiry, and frame another question either to dig into the earlier answer in more depth or to ❂ ❂ ❂

2.	In short, you need to be able to listen, think, and talk ❂ ❂ ❂

3.	At its best, a field research interview is much like normal conversation.

## V.	*Preparing for the Field*

A.	As is true of all research methods, you would be well advised to begin with a search of the relevant literature, filling in your knowledge of the subject and learning what others have said about it.

B.   One of the first steps in preparing for the field is to arrange access to the community corrections agency.

    1.   Obtaining initial approval can be ◕ ◕ ◕   .
    2.   The organization of many criminal justice agencies in large cities is complex, combining a formal hierarchy with a bewildering variety of informal organizational cultures.
    3.   To further complicate field research in criminal justice agencies, the obvious strategy of gaining approval from a single executive—such as a corrections commissioner or police chief—does not guarantee that operations staff at lower levels will cooperate.

VI.   *Access to Formal Organizations*

◇   In any event, your best strategy in gaining access to the community corrections agency, or just about any other formal criminal justice organization, is to use a four-step procedure: ◕ ◕ ◕   .

    1.   *Sponsor:* Your first step is to find a sponsor, a person who is personally known to and respected by the executive director. Ideally, a sponsor will be able to advise you on whom to contact, that person's formal position in the organization, and that person's informal status, including her or his relationships with other key officials.
    2.   *Letter:* Next, write a letter to the executive director. Your letter should have three parts: introduction, brief statement of your research purpose, and action request.
    3.   *Phone Calls:* You probably already know that it can be difficult to arrange meetings with public officials (and often professors), or even to reach people by telephone. You can simplify this task by concluding your letter with a proposal for step 3: arranging a phone call.
    4.   *Meeting:* The final step is meeting with or interviewing the contact person.

VII.   *Access to Subcultures*

A.   Research by Wright and Decker illustrates how gaining access to subcultures in criminal justice—active criminals, deviants, juvenile gangs, inmates—requires tactics that are different in some respects from those used to meet with public officials.

    1.   The basic principle of using a sponsor to gain initial access operates in much the same way, although the word *informant* is normally used to refer to someone who helps make contact with subcultures.
    2.   Informants may be people whose job involves working with criminals: police, juvenile caseworkers, probation officers, attorneys, and counselors at drug clinics are examples.

B.   Whatever techniques are used to identify subjects among subcultures, you should recognize that your sample will ❂ ❂ ❂

      1.   You should also think about potential selection biases in whatever procedures are used to recruit subjects.
      2.   Notice that although we can't make probability statements about samples of active offenders such samples may be representative of a subculture target population.

VIII.   *Selecting Cases for Observation*

     ◇   This brings up the more general question of how cases are selected for observation in field research.

      1.   Often researchers combine the use of informants and what is called **snowball sampling.** Snowball sampling means that initial research subjects (or informants) identify other persons who might also become subjects, who in turn suggest more potential subjects, and so on.
      2.   In such a way, a group of subjects is accumulated through a series of referrals.

IX.   *Sampling in Field Research*

     A.   More generally, the concept of sampling in connection with field research tends to be more complicated than for other kinds of research.

      1.   In many types of field studies, researchers attempt to observe everything within their field of study; thus, in a sense, they do not sample at all. In reality, of course, it is impossible to ❂ ❂ ❂
      2.   The ability to systematically sample cases for observation depends on the degree of structure and predictability of the phenomenon being observed.

     B.   In practice, controlled probability sampling is seldom used in field research. Different types of purposive samples are much more common.

      1.   Nonetheless, understanding the principles and logic of more formal sampling methods is likely to ❂ ❂ ❂

      2.   In field research, bear in mind two stages of sampling. First, to what extent are the total situations available for observation representative of the more general class of phenomena you wish to describe and explain?
      3.   Second, are your actual observations within those total situations representative of all the possible observations?

X.   *Recording Observations*

A.   Just as there is great variety in the types of field studies that might be conducted, many options are available for making records of field observations.

   1.   In conducting field interviews, for example, you will probably write notes of some kind, but you might also ❍ ❍ ❍   .

   2.   Videotaping might also be useful for field interviews to capture visual images of dress and body language.

   3.   Photographs or video tapes can be used to make records of visual images such as a block of apartment buildings before and after some physical design change, or as a pretest for an experimental neighborhood cleanup campaign.

B.   Of course, whatever methods are selected for recording observations are directly related to questions of measurement, especially how key concepts are operationalized.

XI.   *Field Notes*

A.   In many types of field studies, observations are recorded as written notes, perhaps in a ❍ ❍ ❍   .

   1.   Field notes should include both your empirical observations and your interpretations of them.

   2.   You should record what you "know" you have observed and what you "think" you have observed.

   3.   It is important, however, that these different kinds of notes be identified for what they are.

   4.   Some of the most important observations can be anticipated before beginning the study; others will become apparent as your observations progress.

   5.   Sometimes your notetaking can be made easier if you ❍ ❍ ❍   .

B.   Good notetaking requires more careful and deliberate attention and involves some specific skills. Some guidelines follow.

   1.   First, don't trust your memory any more than you have to; it's untrustworthy. It's a good idea to take notes, either ❍ ❍ ❍   .

   2.   Second, it's usually a good idea to take notes in stages. In the first stage, you may need to take sketchy notes (words and phrases) to keep abreast of what's happening. Then get off by yourself and rewrite your notes in more detail.

3. Third, you will inevitably wonder how much you should record. Generally, in field research you can't be really sure of what's important and what's unimportant until you've had a chance to review and analyze a great volume of information, so you should even record things that don't seem important at the outset.

XII. *Structured Observations*

◇ Field notes may also be recorded on highly structured forms, where observers mark items in much the same way a survey interviewer uses a closed-ended questionnaire.

1. Since structured field observation forms often resemble survey questionnaires, use of such forms has the benefit of producing ❂ ❂ ❂

2. The Bureau of Justice Assistance (1993) has produced a handbook for conducting structured field observations, termed **environmental surveys**.

XIII. *Linking Field Observations and Other Data*

A. Although criminal justice research may utilize field methods (or sample surveys) exclusively, it is often the case that a project will collect data from several sources.

B. Field research could also be conducted after ❂ ❂ ❂

1. The flexibility of field methods is one reason why observation and field interviews can readily be incorporated into many research projects.
2. And field observation often confers a much richer understanding of a phenomenon that is imperfectly revealed through a survey questionnaire.

XIV. *Strengths and Weaknesses of Field Research*

A. Field research is especially effective for studying the subtle nuances of behavior and for examining processes over time. For these reasons, the chief strength of this method lies in ❂ ❂ ❂

1. Field studies of behavior are often more appropriate than ❂ ❂ ❂

2. Flexibility is another advantage of field research. Moreover, you are always prepared to engage in qualitative field research, whenever the occasion should arise, whereas launching a survey ❂ ❂ ❂

3. Field research can be relatively inexpensive. This is not to say that field research is never expensive.

B. Field research has a number of weaknesses as well.

    1. First, qualitative studies seldom yield ❂ ❂ ❂

    2. Second, field observation can produce systematic counts of behaviors and reasonable estimates for a large population of behaviors beyond those actually observed. However, since it is not usually possible to know the total population of phenomena—shoppers or drivers, for example—precise probability samples cannot normally be drawn.

C. More generally, the advantages and disadvantages of different types of field studies can be considered in terms of ❂ ❂ ❂

XV. Validity

A. Survey measurements are sometimes criticized as superficial and weak on validity. Observational studies have the potential to ❂ ❂ ❂

B. Validity is a particular strength of field research. As we have pointed out repeatedly, quantitative measurements based on surveys or on simple counts of some phenomenon represent an incomplete picture of the fundamental concept we are interested in.

XVI. Reliability

◇ Qualitative field research, however, does have a potential problem with reliability. Field research measurements—although in-depth—are also often very personal.

XVII. Generalizability

A. One of the chief goals of social science is generalization. We study particular situations and events to learn about life in general.

    1. Usually, nobody would be interested in ❂ ❂ ❂

    2. We are interested only if their victimization experiences can be generalized to all U.S. households.

B. Generalizability can be a problem for qualitative field research.

    1. First, the personal nature of the observations and measurements made by the researcher can produce results that would not necessarily be replicated by another, independent researcher.

    2.   Second, because field researchers get a full and in-depth view of their subject matter, they can reach an unusually comprehensive understanding.

C.   Even quantitative field studies may be weak on generalizability.

KEY NAMES AND TERMS

participant observation
complete participant
participant-as-observer
observer-as-participant
complete observer
field journal
environmental surveys

Multiple Choice Questions

1.   Professor Simpson sits in the back of a court room and takes notes on the facial expressions of jury members during the course of a murder trial. This researcher is playing the role of

    a.   complete participant
    b.   participant-as-observer
    c.   observer-as-participant
    d.   complete observer

2.   Which one of the following methods of recording observation should never be used in field research?

    a.   field notes
    b.   tape recorder
    c.   hidden camera
    d.   all are potentially appropriate methods

3.   A prison inmate is studying for his masters degree in criminal justice. He decides to conduct a study in his cell block on the quality of communication between inmates and correctional officers. He observes inmate-officer interactions as they occur, and takes detailed notes. Neither the inmates nor the correctional officers are aware of the study. This researcher is playing the role of a(n)

    a.   complete participant
    b.   participant-as-observer
    c.   observer-as-participant
    d.   complete observer

4.   Dr. Krishna is interested in the brain-washing techniques used by cult leaders on new members. She pretends to be a depressed loner interested in joining a particular cult. She uses a hidden tape recorder and keeps a field journal to record observations. This researcher is playing the role of a(n)

    a.   complete participant
    b.   participant-as-observer
    c.   observer-as-participant
    d.   complete observer

5.   Which one of the following topics would be least appropriate to field research?

    a.   police officer-suspect interaction during an arrest
    b.   adolescent opinions of police officers
    c.   an examination of crowd-control measures at a rock concert
    d.   looting behavior during a riot

6.   Professor Perez wishes to conduct a study of gang member initiation practices in an East Los Angeles juvenile male gang. The best strategy she could use for gaining access to this subculture would be to

    a.   write a letter to the gang leader, requesting a meeting to discuss the study.
    b.   spend time in the neighborhood in which the gang is located and ask members to participate in the study.
    c.   seek an introduction to the gang by a social worker who is familiar with many of the gang members.
    d.   attempt to disguise herself as a juvenile male interested in joining the gang.

7.   A researcher is interested in studying the behavior of homeless persons. Over the course of one summer, he observes homeless persons in a particular city during daytime working hours. This researcher could have increased the generalizability of this research the most by

        a.   administering questionnaires to the homeless people he observed.
        b.   keeping a field journal of subjective observations.
        c.   considering different sampling dimensions.
        d.   using a video camera to record behavior.

8.   Dr. Vincent conducted a study of marijuana farmers. After being introduced to several of the farmers by an informant, he made a number of visits to a tavern where the growers spend a lot of their time. During these visits, he engaged in directed conversations with the farmers to learn about their activities. This researcher used which one of the following methods for obtaining information?

        a.   structured interviews
        b.   unstructured interviews
        c.   observational interviews
        d.   questionnaires

9.   Which one of the following is not an advantage of field research?

        a.   flexibility
        b.   it can be inexpensive
        c.   increased validity over survey research
        d.   increased reliability over survey research

10.   Which one of the following measures obtained through direct observation is the lest reliable?

        a.   an electronic device counts the number of motorists who pass a particular intersection
        b.   an observer-as-participant counts the number of positive, negative, and neutral encounters between police and citizens
        c.   an observer stands by a particular intersection and counts the number drivers who are not wearing a seat belt.
        d.   an observer counts the number of people who enter a store.

11. It would be easiest to systematically sample cases for observation from which one of the following target populations?

    a. correctional officers
    b. gang members
    c. prostitutes
    d. runaway youth

12. Which one of the following sampling designs would be the most suitable for studying high-paid call-girls?

    a. snowball
    b. systematic
    c. random
    d. multistage cluster

13. Which one of the following statements does not characterize field research?

    a. It is often a theory-generating activity.
    b. It may provide qualitative or quantitative data.
    c. It involves asking questions and direct observation.
    d. It is more valid and reliable than survey research.

True/False Questions

1. Observation is the only reliable method of field research for criminal justice researchers.

    a. true
    b. false

2. It is unethical to deceive subjects solely for the purpose of deception.

    a. true
    b. false

3. Once you have gained formal access to an institution you will automatically have cooperation of the membership of that institution.

    a. true
    b. false

4.   A sampling frame in field research is exactly the same as one in probability sampling.

        a.   true
        b.   false

5.   One useful way of recording information gathered in field studies is by writing notes.

        a.   true
        b.   false

6.   Field observations may be linked to other types of research methods in order to obtain a clearer view of what is being studied.

        a.   true
        b.   false

7.   Qualitative field research is always quite reliable.

        a.   true
        b.   false

8.   Field research is only used in qualitative studies.

        a.   true
        b.   false

9.   It is generally accepted by social science researchers that field research produces findings which are better able to be generalized as compared to many quantitative approaches.

        a.   true
        b.   false

10.   It is sometimes useful to record your field notes directly onto highly structured forms.

        a.   true
        b.   false

Essay Questions

1. You have been hired to study the morale of police officers in your jurisdiction. Discuss the advantages of using field research over other types of research methods. Furthermore, discuss the disadvantages of using field research over other types of research methods. Continue by selecting one method to study this issue and briefly outline the design and data collection procedures that you would use. Finally, compare the various research methods identified with respect to the issues of validity, reliability, and generalizability?

2. Explain how qualitative data can be used to generate theory. Illustrate the process of producing grounded theory with a criminal justice example.

Chapter 12

Agency Records, Content Analysis, and Secondary Data

Chapter Outline

I.   *Introduction*

    A.   A great deal of criminal justice research draws on data collected by state and local agencies such as police, criminal courts, probation offices, juvenile authorities, and corrections departments.

        1.   Federal organization like the FBI, the Bureau of Justice Statistics, the Federal Bureau of Prisons, and the National Institute of Corrections compile information about crime problems and criminal justice institutions.

        2.   In addition, nongovernmental organizations such as the National Center for State Courts and the American Prosecutors' Research Institute collect data from members.

        3.   Government agencies gather a vast amount of crime and criminal justice data, probably rivaled only by efforts to produce economic and public health indicators.

    B.   In *content analysis,* researchers examine ❂ ❂ ❂

    C.   Information collected by others is frequently used in criminal justice research, which in this case involves ❂ ❂ ❂

II. *Topics Appropriate for Agency Records*

    A.   Data from agency records or archives could have been originally gathered in any number of ways, from sample surveys to direct observation. Published statistics and agency records are most commonly used in descriptive or exploratory studies.

        1.   Agency records may also be used in ❂ ❂ ❂

        2.   Agency records are frequently used in ❂ ❂ ❂

        3.   In a different type of applied study, Blumstein, Cohen, and Miller (1980) combined data from prison sentences, arrest rates, and the U.S. Census to develop a mathematical model that predicts future prison populations in Pennsylvania. This is an example of ❂ ❂ ❂

    B.   Topics appropriate to research using content analysis center on the important links between communication, perceptions of crime problems, individual behavior, and criminal justice policy.

C. Research data collected by other investigators, through surveys or field observation may be used for a broad variety of later studies.

    1. Existing data should also be considered at least as a supplemental source of data.

    2. This is not to say that agency records and secondary data can always provide answers to research questions.

III. *Published Statistics*

A. Many government organizations routinely collect and publish compilations of data.

B. The Census Bureau conducts enumerations and sample surveys for several other federal organizations: Notable examples are the NCVS, Census of Children in Custody, Survey of Inmates in Local Jails, Correctional Populations in the United States, and Survey of Justice Expenditure and Employment.

C. The BJS compiles data from several sources and publishes annual and special reports on most data series. For example, Criminal Victimization in the United *States* reports summary data from the NCVS each year.

    1. Annual reports titled *Correctional Populations in the United States* present findings from sample surveys and enumerations of jail, prison, and juvenile facility populations.

    2. *The Prosecution of Felony Arrests* reports detailed data on felony dispositions in selected cities.

    3. The most comprehensive BJS publication on criminal justice data is the annual *Sourcebook of Criminal Justice Statistics*. Since 1972, this report has summarized hundreds of criminal justice data series, ranging from public perceptions about crime, through characteristics of criminal justice agencies, to, in the 1995 report, a table on how states execute capital sentences.

D. At this point, however, we want to suggest some possible uses, and limits, of what Herbert Jacob (1984:9) refers to the accessibility of this multitude of sources as being "like the apple in the Garden of Eden: tempting but full of danger. . .[for] the unwary researcher."

    1. Often, data are presented in highly aggregated form and ❂ ❂ ❂

    2. This is not to say that published data are useless to criminal justice researchers. Highly aggregated summary data from published statistical series are frequently used in descriptive, explanatory, and applied studies.

3. Published data can therefore address questions about highly aggregated patterns or trends--crowding in state prisons, the covariation in two estimates of crime, or epochal change in fatal violence

4. Published data also have the distinct advantage of being readily available; a trip to the library or a letter to the BJS can quickly place several volumes of data series at your disposal.

E. Finally, published data series are available in several media. For example, you can obtain NCVS data through printed reports, microforms, computer tapes, diskettes, and compact disk formats.

F. Of course, before using either original data or tabulations from published sources, you must consider the issues of validity and reliability, and the more general question of how well these data meet your specific research purpose.

IV. Nonpublic Agency Records

A. Despite the large volume of published statistics in criminal justice, such data represent ◐ ◐ ◐   .

1. The FBI publishes the summary UCR, but each of the nation's several thousand law enforcement agencies produces an incredible volume of data not routinely released for public distribution.

2. The BJS publication *Correctional Populations in the United* States, presents statistics on prison inmates collected from annual surveys of correctional facilities, but any given correctional facility maintains detailed case files on individual inmates.

3. The volume *Court Caseload Statistics*, published by the National Center for State Courts, contains summary data on cases filed and disposed in state courts, but any courthouse in any large city houses paper or computer files on thousands of individual defendants.

4. Finally, reports on the annual survey of expenditure and employment in criminal justice are sources of summary data on budgets and personnel, but every agency maintains its own detailed records of expenditures and human resources.

B. Let's consider two of the potential validity and reliability issues that might be raised by using ◐ ◐ ◐   .

1. First, data from juvenile and adult criminal courts reveal only cases of abuse that come to the attention of public officials. Unreported and unsubstantiated cases are not included raising a question about the validity of how many independent variables are measured.

2. Second, dependent variable measures are ◐ ◐ ◐   .

V. *New Data Collected by Agency Staff*

    A.   It is sometimes possible to employ a hybrid source of data in which criminal justice agency staff collect information for specific research purposes. We refer to this as a hybrid source, since it combines the collection of new data--through observation or interviews--with day-to-day criminal justice agency activities.

    B.   Incorporating new data collection into agency routine has two major advantages.

        1.   The most obvious is that having agency staff collect data for you is much less costly than fielding a team of research assistants.

        2.   Second, you have more control over the measurement process than you would by ❂ ❂ ❂   .

    C.   On the other hand, having agencies collect original research data has some disadvantages.

        1.   One obvious one is the need to obtain the cooperation of organizations and staff. The difficulty of this varies in direct proportion to the intrusiveness of data collection.

        2.   You will usually have less control over the data-collection process when ❂ ❂ ❂   .

    D.   Remember to expect the expected; if your findings are not what you expect, look more closely for ❂ ❂ ❂   .

VI. *Units of Analysis*

    A.   As we mentioned earlier in this chapter, archives and agency records may be based on units of analysis that are not suitable for particular research questions.

        1.   If you are interested in studying individual probationers, for example, you would require individual-level data about persons sentenced to probation.

        2.   A general rule we mentioned in Chapter 4 bears repeating here: it is possible to move from individual to aggregate units of analysis, but not the other way around.

        3.   If you will use agency records, you must be attentive to the match or mismatch between the units of analysis required to address your specific research questions and the level of aggregation represented in agency records.

        4.   Defining individual people as units can resolve the conceptual problems that emerge from complex relationships between different units of count.

VII.   *Sampling*

    ◇   It may sometimes be appropriate to select subsets of agency records for particular research purposes.

        ◇   You will be glad to hear that once units of analysis are defined, sampling agency records is relatively simple. In most cases, a target population and sample frame may be readily defined.

VIII.   *Reliability and Validity*

    A.   The key to evaluating the reliability and validity of agency records, as well as the general suitability of those data for a research project, is to understand as completely as possible ❂ ❂ ❂

        1.   You should also recognize the importance of understanding how such records are produced.
        2.   You will also be better able to anticipate and detect potential reliability or validity problems in agency records.

    B.   Users of data series collected over time must be especially attentive to changes in data-collection procedures or changes in operational definitions for key indicators.

        1.   Such changes are more likely to occur in ❂ ❂ ❂

        2.   The longitudinal researcher must therefore diligently search for modifications of procedures or definitions over time in order to avoid attributing some substantive meaning to change in a particular measure.
        3.   Furthermore, as the time interval under investigation increases, so does the potential for change in measurement.
        4.   Researchers who analyze criminal justice data produced by different cities or states or other jurisdictions must be alert to variations in definitions and measurement of key variables.
        5.   Fortunately, most published reports on regular data series present ❂ ❂ ❂

IX.   *Sources of Reliability and Validity Problems*

    A.   Virtually all criminal justice recordkeeping is a social process. By this we mean that indicators of arrest, juvenile probation violations, court convictions, or rule infractions by prison inmates reflect decisions made by criminal justice officials in addition to the actual behavior of juvenile or adult offenders.

◇ "Researchers must realize that performance measures are composites of offenders' behavior, organizational capacity to detect behavior, and decisions about how to respond to offenders' misbehavior."

B. Discretionary actions by criminal justice officials and others affect the production of ◉ ◉ ◉   .

C. In many cases, criminal justice officials collect data because the law requires them to do so. Even more generally, agencies most commonly collect data for their own use, not for the use of researchers.

D. The general point is that your research needs may not be congruent with agency recordkeeping practices.

    1. Courts or police departments may use idiosyncratic definitions or methods of classifying information that make such records difficult to use.

    2. Also recognize that your conceptual and operational definitions of key concepts, however thoughtful and precise, will seldom be identical to actual measures maintained by criminal justice agencies.

E. At the operational level, most officials in criminal justice organizations are more interested in keeping track of individual cases than they are in examining patterns.

F. There is a greater potential for clerical errors as ◉ ◉ ◉   .

G. The relationship between the volume of data entry and the potential for error can be especially troublesome for studies of relatively rare crimes of incidents.

X. *Content Analysis*

A. Content analysis methods may be applied to ◉ ◉ ◉   .

    1. First, you develop operational definitions of the key variables in your inquiry: For examples, men's products and violence.

    2. Next, you'd have to decide what to watch. Probably you would decide (l) what stations to watch, (2) for what days or period, and (3) at what hours.

    3. Once you had completed your observations, you'd be able to analyze the data you collected and determine whether men's product manufacturers sponsored more blood and gore than other sponsors.

B. Content analysis, then, is particularly well suited to the study of communications and to answering the classic question of communications research: " Who says what, ◉ ◉ ◉   ?"

XI.   *Units of Analysis and Sampling in Content Analysis*

    A.   In the study of communications, as in the study of people, it is usually impossible to directly observe all you are interested in.

        1.   Usually, then, it's ◐ ◑ ◐

    B.   The complexity of determining appropriate units of analysis is often more apparent in content analysis than in other research methods.

    C.   In designing the sample, you would need to establish the universe to be sampled from.

    D.   Once you have become clear about your units of analysis and the observations appropriate to those units and have created a sampling frame like the one illustrated, sampling is simple and straightforward.

XII.   *Coding in Content Analysis*

    A.   Content analysis is essentially a coding operation, and, of course, coding represents ◐ ◑ ◐

        1.   Communications--oral, written, or other--are coded or classified according to some ◐ ◑ ◐
        2.   Recall that coded terms are subject to many interpretations, and the researcher must specify definitions clearly.

    B.   Coding in content analysis involves the logic of conceptualization and operationalization as discussed in Chapter 5.

        1.   In content analysis, as in other research methods, you must refine your conceptual framework and develop specific methods for observing in relation to that framework.
        2.   For all research methods, conceptualization and operationalization typically involve ◐ ◑ ◐

    C.   As in other decisions relating to measurement, the researcher faces a fundamental choice between depth and specificity of understanding. The content analyst has a choice between searching for manifest or latent content.

        1.   Coding the manifest content--the visible, surface content--of a communication more closely approximates the use of closed-ended items in a survey questionnaire.
        2.   Alternatively, you may code the latent content of the communication: its ◐ ◑ ◐

3. In the most general sense, manifest and latent content can be distinguished by the degree of interpretation required in measurement.

D. Throughout the process of conceptualizing manifest-and latent-content coding procedures, you should remember that the operational definition of any variable is composed of the attributes included in it.

    1. Such attributes, moreover, should ◐ ◐ ◐   .
    2. No coding scheme should be used in content analysis until it has been carefully pretested.
    3. You should review the overall results of the pretest to ensure they will be appropriate to your analytic concerns.

E. Before beginning to code newspapers, crime dramas on TV, or detective fiction, you should also make plans to assess coding reliability.

    1. First, intercoder reliability can be determined by having two different people code the same message and computing the proportion of items coded the same by each person.
    2. The second way to assess coding reliability is the test-retest method, in which one person codes the same message twice.

XIII. *Secondary Analysis*

    ◇ Secondary Analysis encompasses all other sources of criminal justice data we have described in this and preceding chapters--content analysis, agency records, field observation and surveys.

XIV. *Advantages and Disadvantages of Secondary Data*

A. The advantages of secondary analysis are obvious and enormous.

    1. It is cheaper and faster than collecting original data.
    2. Depending on who did the original study, you ◐ ◐ ◐

B. There are disadvantages, however.

    ◇ The key problem involves the recurrent question of validity. When one researcher collects data for one particular purpose, you have no assurance that those data will be appropriate to your research interests.

C.   In general, secondary data are least ● ● ●

        1.   This is the case because evaluations are designed to answer specific questions about specific programs.

        2.   It is always possible to reanalyze data from evaluations studies, but secondary data cannot be used to evaluate an entirely different program.

Key Terms

content analysis
secondary analysis

Multiple Choice Questions

1.   A researcher is interested in studying the budgeting of money within a police department in a mid-sized American city. She gains access to the department's detailed records of expenditures and human resources. This is an example of which type of agency records, as described in the text?

      a.   published statistics.
      b.   nonpublic agency records.
      c.   new data collected by agency staff.
      d.   none of the above.

2.   Dr. Glynn wishes to analyze Saturday morning cartoons to see whether more violent actions involve cats or dogs. The form of data collection most suited to this topic is

      a.   secondary data analysis.
      b.   media record analysis.
      c.   content analysis.
      d.   nonpublic agency records analysis.

3.   Dr. Lawrence Review is interested in using data collected by a research group in Denmark to examine an original research question related to the criminal behavior of identical twins. This type of research is referred to as

      a.   secondary data analysis
      b.   content analysis
      c.   foreign record analysis
      d.   hybrid data analysis

4. Secondary data analysis is least appropriate for which one of the following types of research?

    a.   explanatory
    b.   exploratory
    c.   evaluation
    d.   description

5. Content analysis may be applied to which one of the following?

    a.   nonverbal communication
    b.   court transcripts
    c.   history books
    d.   all are appropriate applications

6. Which attributes could reflect the latent content of a letter to the editor?

    a.   belligerent or not
    b.   more than 200 words or not
    c.   number of times "I" is mentioned
    d.   signed by a male, female, or anonymous

7. Which of the following is not a source of reliability and validity problems with agency data? (You may choose more than one response.)

    a.   changes in definitions of crime over time
    b.   agency data are not designed for research
    c.   agency data are designed to track patterns, not people
    d.   data entry errors

8. Dr. Wishman obtained a published report on state inmate populations during the years 1980-1990. Which one of the following would not be an appropriate research question?

    a.   Did the number of inmates in prisons in Southern states increase at a higher rate than in Northern states during the years 1980-1990?
    b.   Which state had the greatest number of inmates during 1990?
    c.   Do inmates sentenced for drug crimes have more conduct violations than inmates sentenced for property crimes?
    d.   What is the net change in the inmate population for the U.S. between the years 1980 and 1990?

9. The FBI's Uniform Crime Reports are an example of which type of data?

   a. new data collected by agency staff
   b. published statistics
   c. content analysis data
   d. nonpublic agency records

10. Dr. Anderson is interested in studying the amount of overtime worked by police officers. He gains access to agency personnel files. This is an illustration of which type of data?

   a. new data collected by agency staff
   b. nonpublic agency records
   c. secondary data
   d. published statistics

11. The advantages of using secondary data analysis include which of the following? (You may choose more than one response.)

   a. It is the most reliable data.
   b. This method assures validity of your measures.
   c. It is inexpensive
   d. It is easily obtained

12. You are asked to conduct an evaluation of a new drug treatment program in your city. Which of the following types of data would be least appropriate to use for this purpose?

   a. secondary data
   b. nonpublished agency data
   c. published statistics
   d. new data collected by agency staff

13. The ICPSR is the best source of

   a. nonpublished agency data
   b. published statistics
   c. secondary data
   d. hybrid data

14.   Dr. Gamziukas is interested in examining the city of origin of homeless persons who visit a New York City shelter. Unfortunately, the shelter does not ask this information of the clients. This researcher asks shelter staff if they would collect this information at the time of the regular intake interview. The staff agree and after a one-year period, Dr. Gamziukas has her data. Which type of data does this research illustrate?

a.   secondary data
b.   published statistics
c.   nonpublished agency data
d.   new data collected by agency staff

True/False Questions

1.   A great deal of criminal justice research draws on data collected by state and local law enforcement agencies.

a.   true
b.   false

2.   Using content analysis, researchers examine a class of social artifacts.

a.   true
b.   false

3.   Repetition analysis involves the reanalysis of information already collected by others, and is often used in criminal justice research.

a.   true
b.   false

4.   It is not recommended that agency records be used in explanatory studies.

a.   true
b.   false

5.   It is sometimes possible for researchers to convince criminal justice agency staff to collect information for specific research purposes. Maxfield and Babbie refer to this as a hybrid source of data.

a.   true
b.   false

6. One strength of using hybrid data collection techniques is that the researchers gain complete control over what data is collected, especially the data collected by the staff.

   a. true
   b. false

7. A general rule of thumb when analyzing agency data is to "expect the expected".

   a. true
   b. false

8. Archive and agency records are useful for many reasons since the researcher does not need to consider the unit of analysis.

   a. true
   b. false

9. It may sometimes be appropriate to select subsets of agency records for particular research purposes.

   a. true
   b. false

10. Researchers must realize that performance measures are composites of offenders' behavior, organizational capacity to detect behavior, and decisions about how to respond to offenders' misbehavior.

    a. true
    b. false

Essay Questions

1. Discuss the three categories of information collected for or by public agencies. How do they compare in the areas of availability to researchers and degree of researcher control over material?

2. Explain the differences between latent content and manifest content. Consider the example of a letter to the editor in a local paper. If you were conducting a content analysis of letters to the editor, describe something about a letter that would be coded as latent content and something that would be coded as manifest content. Which approach is generally considered to provide be more reliable? Explain. Which approach is generally considered to be more valid. Explain.

Chapter 13

PROGRAM EVALUATION AND POLICY ANALYSIS

Chapter Outline

I.   *Introduction*

    ◇   Evaluation research—sometimes called program evaluation—refers to ❂ ❂ ❂ .

        1.   Its special purpose is to evaluate the impact of interventions such as mandatory arrest for domestic violence, innovations in probation, new sentencing laws, and a wide variety of such programs.

        2.   Other types of evaluation studies—policy analysis—are designed to ❂ ❂ ❂ .

        3.   Many methods, including surveys, experiments, and so on, can be used in evaluation research and policy analysis.

II. *Topics Appropriate for Evaluation Research and Policy Analysis*

    ◇   Most fundamentally, evaluation research is appropriate ❂ ❂ ❂ .

        1.   A policy intervention is an action taken for the purpose of producing some intended result.

        2.   In its simplest sense, evaluation research is a process of determining whether ❂ ❂ ❂ .

III. *The Policy Process*

    A.   The policy process begins with some demand that normally appears as support for some new course of action or opposition to existing policy.

    B.   The next step actually encompasses several steps.

        1.   Policymakers consider ultimate goals they wish to accomplish and different actions for achieving those goals.

        2.   Since the word *policy* implies some standard course of action about how to respond to some recurring problem or issue, routine practices and decision rules must be formulated.

3. Policy outputs refer to what is actually produced, in much the same manner that a manufacturer of office supplies produces paper clips and floppy disks.

C. In the final stage, we consider the ❶ ❷ ❸ .

D. The distinction between policy outputs and their impacts is important for understanding applications of evaluation to different stages of the policy process.

 1. Impacts are fundamentally related to policy goals, referring to the basic question of what a policy action is ❶ ❷ ❸ .
 2. Outputs embody the means to achieve desired policy goals.

E. Policies are formulated to produce some effect or impact.

 1. In this sense, a policy can be viewed as a hypothesis in which an independent variable is expected to produce change in some dependent variable.
 2. Goal-directed public polices may therefore be viewed as *if-then statements*: if: if some policy action is taken, then we expect some result to be produced.

IV. *Linking the Process to Evaluation*

A. Note that policy analysis, as we have described it, takes places in the policymaking stage. In contrast, program evaluation studies are conducted in later stages, seeking the answers to two types of questions:

 1. Are policies being ❶ ❷ ❸ ?
 2. Are policies achieving their intended goals?
 3. Evaluation, therefore, seeks to link the intended actions and goals of criminal justice policy to empirical evidence that policies are being carried out as planned and that they are having the desired effects.

B. Ideally, impact assessments and process evaluations are ❶ ❷ ❸ .

V. *Getting Started*

 ✧ Several steps are involved in planning any type of research project, as we discussed in Chapter 4.

 1. You need to think about design, measurement, sampling, data-collection procedures, analysis, and so on.

2.   You also have to address such practical problems as obtaining access to people, information, and data needed in an evaluation.

VI.   *Evaluability Assessment*

◇   An *evaluability assessment* is described by Rossi and Freeman (1993:145) as sort of a "preevaluation," where a researcher determines whether requisite conditions for conducting an evaluation are present.

1.   One obvious condition is support for the study from organizations delivering program components that will be evaluated.
2.   What are general ❂ ❂ ❂   ?
3.   How are these goals translated into program components?
4.   What kinds of records and data are readily available?
5.   Do other persons or organizations have some sort of ❂ ❂ ❂
                                                                        ?

VII.   *Problem Formulation*

A.   We mentioned above that evaluation research questions may be defined for you. This is true in a general sense, but formulating applied research problems that can be empirically evaluated is an important and often difficult step.

1.   To conduct evaluation research, we must be able to ❂ ❂ ❂
                                                                        .

2.   This process normally begins by identifying and specifying program goals.

B.   The different organizations involved in an evaluation represent multiple stakeholders—persons and organizations that had some stake in the program.

1.   These different stakeholders often have different goals and different views on how a program should actually operate.
2.   Clearly specifying program goals, then, is a fundamental first step in conducting evaluation studies.
3.   If there is uncertainty about what a program is expected to achieve, it is not possible to determine whether goals are reached.
4.   Or, if multiple stakeholders embrace different goals, evaluators must ❂ ❂ ❂
                                                                        .

VIII. Measurement

A. After identifying program goals, your attention should turn to measurement, considering first how to measure a program's success in meeting goals.

    1. "For evaluation purposes, goal setting must lead to the operationalization of the desired outcome; that is, the condition to be dealt with must be specified in detail, together with one or more measurable criteria of success. Evaluation researchers often refer to these operationalized statements as *objectives*"

    2. Obtaining evaluable statements of program goals is conceptually similar to the measurement process, where program objectives represent conceptual definitions of what a program is trying to accomplish.

B. Notice, however, that although outcome measures are derived from goals, they are ❍❍❍   .

    1. Program goals represent *desired outcomes*, while outcome measures are empirical indicators of ❍❍❍   .

    2. Furthermore, if a program pursues multiple goals, researchers may have to either devise multiple outcome measures or select a subset of possible measures to correspond with a subset of goals.

    3. You specify an operational definition by describing empirical indicators of program outcomes.

C. Measuring the dependent variables directly involved in an impact assessment is only a beginning.

    1. It is often appropriate and important to measure aspects of the context within which the program is conducted.

    2. These variables are external to the experiment itself, yet they affect it.

D. Besides making measurements relevant to the outcomes of a program, it is also necessary to measure the program intervention—the experimental stimulus or independent variable.

E. It is usually necessary to measure the population of subjects involved in the program being evaluated.

    1. In particular, it is important to define those for whom the program is appropriate.

2.   In evaluation studies, such persons are referred to as a program's ● ● ● .

F.   This process of definition and measurement has two aspects.

    1.   First, the program target population must be specified. Evaluators consult program officials to identify the intended targets or beneficiaries of a particular program.

    2.   Most evaluation studies that use individual people as units of analysis will also measure such background variables as age, sex, educational attainment, employment history, prior criminal record, and so forth.

    3.   Second, in providing for the measurement of these different kinds of variables, there is a continuing choice—whether to create new measures or use ones that are already being collected in the course of normal program operation.

    4.   Since we are talking about measurement here, your decision to use your own measures or those produced by agencies should be based on ● ● ● .

G.   As you can see, measurement must be taken very seriously in evaluation research. You must carefully determine all the variables to be measured and get appropriate measures for each.

IX.   *Randomized Evaluation Designs*

A.   One of the most important benefits of randomization is to avoid the selectivity (selection bias) that is such a fundamental part of criminal justice decision making.

    1.   Police selectively arrest people, prosecutors selectively file charges, judges and juries selectively convict defendants, and offenders are selectively punished.

    2.   In a more general sense, randomization is the great equalizer: through probability theory we can assume that groups created by random assignment will be ● ● ● .

B.   On the other hand, randomized designs are not suitable for evaluating all experimental criminal justice programs.

C.   Random assignment of people to receive some especially desirable or punitive treatment may not be possible for legal, ● ● ● .

D.   In any real-world delivery of alternative programs or treatments to victims, offenders, or criminal justice agency staff, exceptions to random assignment are all but inevitable.

E.　However, as the number of exceptions to random assignment increases, the statistical equivalence of experimental and control groups is threatened.

　　1.　You should recognize that when police (or others) make exceptions to random assignment, they are introducing bias in the selection of ❂ ❂ ❂ .

　　2.　Randomized experiments are best suited for programs where such exceptions can be minimized.

F.　In Chapter 9, we explained the relationship between sample size and accuracy in estimating population characteristics. As sample size increases (up to a point), estimates of population means and standard errors become more precise.

　　1.　By the same token, the number of subjects in groups created through random assignment is related to the researcher's ability to detect significant differences in outcome measures between groups.
　　2.　If there is only a small number of subjects in each group, statistical tests can detect only very large program effects or differences in outcome measures between the two groups.

G.　Caseflow represents the ❂ ❂ ❂ .

H.　Treatment integrity refers to whether an experimental intervention is delivered as intended. Sometimes called *treatment consistency*, treatment integrity is therefore roughly equivalent to measurement reliability.

I.　Midstream changes in experimental programs can also threaten treatment integrity.

　　1.　Rossi and Freeman (1993:290) point out that the possibility of midstream changes means that randomized designs are usually not appropriate for evaluating programs in early stages of development where such changes are more likely.
　　2.　If you detect differences in outcome measures between experimental and control groups, you would not know how much of the difference might be due to the midstream change.

J.　Randomized experiments therefore require that certain conditions be met.

　　1.　Staff responsible for program delivery must accept random assignment and further agree to minimize exceptions to randomization.
　　2.　Caseflow must be adequate to produce enough subjects in each group so that statistical tests will be able to detect significant differences in outcome measures.

3.   Finally, experimental interventions must be ❂ ❂ ❂

K.   These conditions, and the problems that can result if they are not met, can be summarized as two overriding concerns in field experiments:

1.   Equivalence between experimental and control groups ❂ ❂ ❂

2.   Ability to detect differences in outcome measures after an intervention is introduced.

X.   *Quasi-Experimental Designs*

A.   Quasi-experiments are distinguished from "true" experiments by the ❂ ❂ ❂

1.   Achieving random assignment of subjects is often impossible in criminal justice evaluations

2.   Quasi-experiments may also be "nested" into experimental designs as backups should one or more of the requisites for a true experiment break down.

B.   Often, a researcher or public official may decide to conduct an evaluation sometime after an experimental program has gone into effect. Such situations are referred to as *ex post evaluations* (Rossi and Freeman, 1993:300) and are not usually amenable to introducing random assignment after the fact.

C.   Interventions such as new national or statewide laws are examples of full-coverage programs where it is not possible to identify subjects who are not exposed to the intervention, let alone randomly assign persons to receive or not receive the treatment.

D.   Similarly, some experimental interventions may be designed to affect all persons in some larger unit—a neighborhood crime prevention program, for example.

E.   Quasi-experimental designs lack the built-in controls for selection bias and other ❂ ❂ ❂

1.   Nonequivalent-groups designs, by definition, cannot be assumed to include treatment and comparison subjects who are statistically equivalent.

2.   For evaluation designs that use nonequivalent groups, your attention should be devoted to constructing experimental and comparison groups that are as similar as possible on important variables that might account for differences in outcome measures.

F.　Interrupted time-series designs require attention to different issues, since researchers cannot normally control how reliably the experimental treatment is actually implemented. Foremost among these are ❂ ❂ ❂.

◇　In many interrupted time-series designs, conclusions about whether an intervention produced change in some outcome measure rely on simple indicators that represent complex causal processes.

G.　Understanding the causal process that produces measures used in time-series analysis is crucial for interpreting results. Such understanding can come in two related ways.

1.　First, you should have a sound conceptual grasp of the underlying causal forces at work in whatever process you are interested in.
2.　Second, you should understand ❂ ❂ ❂.

XI.　*Nonexperimental Evaluation Studies*

A.　Random assignment, the ability to manipulate an experimental intervention, and other controls over experimental conditions are the general hallmarks of ❂ ❂ ❂.

B.　In many cases, useful evaluations may be performed even if requirements for experimental or quasi-experimental designs cannot be met.

1.　This is also true for evaluations initially designed with more rigorous experimental conditions that cannot be maintained.
2.　Nonexperimental evaluations, or case studies, may provide useful information to policymakers and other public officials.

C.　Whenever possible, randomized or quasi-experimental evaluations ❂ ❂ ❂.

1.　When this is not possible, a salvage evaluation or case study ❂ ❂ ❂.

2.　Case studies can sometimes be designed to satisfy the definition of program evaluation we quoted at the beginning of this chapter, by systematically applying social science research procedures to examine some individual program or agency.

D. Our general advice in this regard is simple: do the best you can. Doing this requires two things:

    1. Understanding the strengths and limits of social science research procedures.
    2. Carefully diagnosing what is needed and what is possible in some particular application.

XII. *Other Types of Evaluation Studies*

A. Process evaluations can be invaluable aids in ❂ ❂ ❂

B. Process evaluations can also be useful for criminal justice officials whose responsibility centers more on ❂ ❂ ❂

C. So process evaluations can be valuable in their own right, as well as important for diagnosing measures of program effects.

XIII. *Policy Analysis*

◇ Program evaluation differs from policy analysis with respect to the time dimension and where each activity takes place in the policy process.

    1. Policy analysis is used to ❂ ❂ ❂

    2. Because of this, policy analysis is a more future-oriented activity that frequently produces predictions, while most evaluation studies produce explanations.

XIV. *Modeling Prison Populations*

A. Growth in state and federal prison populations through the 1980s and 1990s caught many public officials only partly by surprise.

    1. For years, researchers such as Alfred Blumstein have used mathematical models to ❂ ❂ ❂
    2. More important, such models permit corrections officials and others to answer "what-if" questions about future prison populations.

B. Model projections are based on data that represent the following:

    1. Demographic structure of ◉ ◉ ◉
    2. Arrest rates broken down by demographic groups
    3. Conviction and incarceration rates broken down ◉ ◉ ◉

C. The pieces of information needed to project prison populations are:

    1. Predictions of future state population, broken down by age groups, sex, and race
    2. Past data on arrest rates for each demographic group, broken down by type of crime
    3. Past data on conviction rates for persons arrested in each crime group
    4. Past data on incarceration rates and imposed sentence length for persons convicted in each crime group
    5. Past data on parole release rates.

D. Prison population models are clearly useful tools for policymakers.

    1. You should recognize that the accuracy of forecasts diminishes with how far into the future they attempt to project, since intentional or unintentional policy changes may alter the flow of persons through courts to prison.
    2. In practice, the conditional probability estimates that form the core of projection models are regularly updated to reflect changes in arrest, conviction, and incarceration rates.

XV. *Political Context of Applied Research*

A. Applied researchers bridge the gap between the body of research knowledge about crime and the practical needs of criminal justice professionals.

B. You will recognize similarities between this material and our discussion of ethics in Chapter 8.

    1. Although ethics and politics are often closely intertwined, the ethics of criminal justice research deals more with the methods employed, while political issues are more concerned with the substance and use of research.
    2. Ethical and political aspects of applied research are also distinct in that there are no formal codes of accepted political conduct comparable to the codes of ethical conduct we discussed earlier.

XVI.   *Evaluation and Stakeholders*

A.   Any applied study will usually involve multiple stakeholders—people who have some direct or indirect interest in the program or evaluation results.

1.   Some stakeholders may be enthusiastic supporters of an experimental program, others may oppose it, while still other stakeholders may be neutral.
2.   Different stakeholder interests in programs can produce conflicting perspectives on evaluations of those programs.

B.   Your best advice in dealing with such problems is twofold.

1.   First, identify program stakeholders, their perspectives on the program, and ❶ ❷ ❸   .
2.   The second step is to educate stakeholders on why an evaluation should be conducted. This is best done by explaining that applied research is conducted to determine what works and what does not.

KEY NAMES AND TERMS

evaluability assessment	evaluation research
evaluation apprehension	treatment integrity
target population	process evaluations
treatment consistency	policy analysis
ex post evaluations	stakeholders

Multiple Choice Questions

1.   Program evaluation differs from policy analysis with respect to

a.   time dimension within the policy process.
b.   cost.
c.   the role of stakeholders.
d.   the role of measurement.

2.   Nesting a quasi-experimental design within a randomized experiment refers to

a.   a way of backing up a true experiment.
b.   using a randomized quasi-experiment to replace a true experiment.
c.   conducting an evaluation some time after an experimental program has gone into effect.
d.   a way to study all people in a certain neighborhood.

3. A process evaluation focuses on

    a. program effects.
    b. random assignment.
    c. implementation.
    d. due process in court proceedings.

4. Evaluability assessment is done to

    a. determine program effects.
    b. determine program costs.
    c. determine whether an evaluation should be conducted.
    d. provide political support for policy analysis.

5. Professor White is interested in conducting an evaluation study of an in-prison treatment program to reduce violent recidivism. He chooses to compare the recidivism rates of the treated prisoners with the recidivism rates of a similar group of prisoner sin another prison. which design would be most suitable for this evaluation?

    a. interrupted time-series
    b. classical experiment
    c. nonequivalent-groups
    d. panel study

6. Dr. Stanley is conducting an evaluation of a new program involving decisions made by parole officers. the ideal design for avoiding selection bias in such programs is

    a. randomized
    b.   nonequivalent groups
    c. ex post
    d. interrupted time-series

7. Treatment integrity refers to

    a. the extent of political bias in an evaluation study
    b. the validity of the treatment
    c. the extent of inconsistencies in treatment
    d. the effectiveness of a treatment

8. Which of the following can threaten treatment integrity?

   a. midstream changes in experimental programs
   b. control group subjects start to receive treatment
   c. researchers are influenced by political pressures to choose a particular type of treatment for study
   d. some members in the treatment group receive less treatment than they are supposed to

9. Professor Nomed is called upon by the National Institute of Justice to conduct an evaluation of an experimental community policing program that stared six months ago. This type of evaluation is referred to as a(n)

   a. delayed evaluation
   b. ex post evaluation
   c. posttest evaluation
   d. none of the above—evaluation is impossible after a program begins

10. Which of the following is not an example of situational crime prevention?

    a. the use of caller ID as a way to reduce obscene phone calls
    b. posting uniformed guards at store entrances to prevent shoplifting
    c. the use of marked patrol cars parked on the side of highways to reduce speeding
    d. stiffer sentencing practices to deter burglary

11. A new law that set the speed limit in all states to 65 miles per hour is an example of

    a. situational crime prevention
    b. full coverage program
    c. ex post intervention
    d. quasi-experimental intervention

12. Which one of the following designs would you choose to evaluate the effect of the above change, if you were restricted to collecting data in one state only?

    a. classic experimental
    b. panel study
    c. non-equivalent groups
    d. interrupted time series

13. Process evaluations

    a.   assess the extent to which policies achieve their intended goals
    b.   focus on policy demands and agenda
    c.   assess the extent to which policies are being implemented as planned
    d.   are essentially the same as impact assessment

14. A study examines whether property values go down after a prison is built in the community. Which type of program evaluation does this example illustrate?

    a.   evaluability assessment
    b.   policy analysis
    c.   impact assessment
    d.   process evaluation

15. Dr. Brown is interested in conducting an evaluation of a new educational program for inner-city preschoolers. Before starting the evaluation, dr. Brown should conduct which one of the following?

    a.   impact assessment
    b.   process evaluation
    c.   ex post evaluation
    d.   evaluability assessment

True/False Questions

1. Evaluation research is a matter of finding out whether something is there or not there, or whether something happened or didn't happen.

    a.   true
    b.   false

2. It is not important to specify program goals in order to evaluate them.

    a.   true
    b.   false

3. A way of measuring program context for an employment program would be to look at the overall job market for the area being studied.

    a.   true
    b.   false

4.	Random assignment of subject must be done in order to produce usable criminal justice research.

	a.	true
	b.	false

5.	Full coverage programs such as the implementation of determinant sentencing laws are good candidates for quasi-experimental research design.

	a.	true
	b.	false

6.	Program evaluation is the same as policy analysis.

	a.	true
	b.	false

7.	Political context is not important in applied research.

	a.	true
	b.	false

8.	The policy process begins with some demand that normally appears as support for some new course of action or opposition to existing policy.

	a.	true
	b.	false

9.	Treatment integrity refers to the process through which subjects are treated in the experimental and control groups.

	a.	true
	b.	false

10.	Quasi-experimental designs lack the built-in controls for selection bias and other threats to internal validity.

	a.	true
	b.	false

Essay Questions

1. Describe how policy analysis can be used in program evaluations. Then, describe how program evaluations can be used in policy analysis. Illustrate your answers with a criminal justice example.

2. Compare and contrast experimental and quasi-experimental designs as they are used to evaluate programs and policies. Supply a strength of each and provide an example that will illustrate the strength selected. Next, supply a weakness of each and provide an example that will illustrate the weakness selected. Finally, in a perfect criminal justice researchers world, which would you prefer to use. Why.

Chapter 14

Interpreting Data

Chapter Outline

I. *Introduction*

    A.   Empirical research is first and foremost a logical rather than ❂ ❂ ❂

        1.   Mathematics is merely a convenient and efficient language for accomplishing the logical operations inherent in good data analysis.

        2.   Statistics is the applied branch of mathematics especially appropriate to a variety of research analyses.

    B.   We'll be looking at two types of statistics: descriptive and ❂ ❂ ❂

        1.   **Descriptive statistics** is a medium for ❂ ❂ ❂

        2.   **Inferential statistics**, on the other hand, assists you in forming conclusions from your observations; typically, that involves ❂ ❂ ❂

II. *Descriptive Statistics*

    A.   Descriptive statistics is a method for ❂ ❂ ❂

        1.   Sometimes we want to describe single variables: this procedures is known as *univariate analysis*. At other times we want to describe the associations that ❂ ❂ ❂

        2.   *Bivariate analysis* refers to descriptions of two variables, while *multivariate analysis* examines relationships among ❂ ❂ ❂

III. *Univariate Analysis*

    A.   **Univariate analysis** is the examination of the distribution of cases on only one variable at a time.

    B.   **Distributions** The most basic format for presenting univariate data is to report all individuals cases--that is, to list the ❂ ❂ ❂

1. Frequency distributions
2. Percentages

C. *Central Tendency*

Beyond simply reporting marginals, you may choose to present your data in the form of summary **averages** or measures of *central tendency*. Your options in this regard are:

1. The **mode** (the most frequent attribute, either grouped or ungrouped).
2. The arithmetic **mean** (average), or the **median** (the middle attribute in the ranked distribution of observed attributes).
3. The easiest average to calculate is the *mode*, the most frequent value.
4. The *median* represents the "middle" value: half are above it, half below.

D. The simplest measure of dispersion is the range: the distance ❿ ❿ ❿
.

E. A somewhat more sophisticated measure of dispersion is the **standard deviation**, which might also be described as the average amount of variation about the mean.

1. That is, if the mean is the average value of all observations in a group, the standard deviation represents ❿ ❿ ❿
.

2. The standard deviation measure of dispersion is based on the squared deviation from the mean.
3. The sum of squared deviations from the mean divided by the number of cases--is known as ❿ ❿ ❿
.
4. Taking the square root of the variance produces the standard deviation.
5. Comparing the relative values for the standard deviation and the mean indicates how much variation there is in a group of cases, relative to the average.
7. Similarly, comparing standard deviations for different groups of cases indicates relative amounts of dispersion within each group.
8. In addition to providing a summary measure of dispersion, the standard deviation plays a role in the calculation of other descriptive statistics.
9. Furthermore, the standard deviation is a central component of many inferential statistics used to make generalizations from a sample of observations to the population from which the sample was drawn.

F. Many other measures of dispersion can help you interpret measures of central tendency.

214

1.   One useful indicator that expresses both dispersion and grouping of cases is the *percentile*, ◑ ◑ ◑

2.   Percentiles may also be grouped into quartiles, expressing cases that fall in the first (lowest), third, and fourth (highest) quarter of a distribution.

G.   Age and the number of prior arrests are continuous, ratio variables; they increase steadily in tiny fractions instead of jumping from category to category as does a discrete variable such as <u>gender</u> or marital status.

    ✧   Strictly speaking, medians and means should be calculated only for ◑ ◑ ◑

H.   **Rates** of things are fundamental descriptive statistics in criminal justice research.

1.   In most cases, rates are used to ◑ ◑ ◑

2.   For example, computing rates enables us to standardize by population size and make more meaningful comparisons.

I.   The arithmetic of calculating rates could not be much easier. What is not so simple, and in any event requires careful consideration, is deciding on the basic two components of rates: numerator and denominator.

1.   The numerator represents the central concept you are interested in measuring, so selection of the numerator involves all the considerations of measurement we have discussed elsewhere.
2.   Choosing the right denominator sometimes presents problems. In most cases, you compute rates to standardize by ◑ ◑ ◑

J.   In presenting univariate--and other--data, you will be constrained by two often conflicting goals.

1.   On the one hand, you should attempt to provide your reader with ◑ ◑ ◑

2.   On the other hand, the data should be presented in a manageable form.

IV.   *Subgroup Comparisons*

A.   Univariate analyses describe the units of analysis of a study and, if they are a sample drawn from some larger population, allow us to make descriptive inference about the larger population.

B.   Bivariate and multivariate analyses are aimed primarily at ◑ ◑ ◑

V.   *Bivariate Analysis*

A.   In contrast to univariate analysis, subgroup comparisons constitute a kind of **bivariate analysis** in that two variables are involved.

1.   The purpose of subgroup comparisons is also largely descriptive-- independently describing the subgroups--but the element of comparison is added.
2.   Most bivariate analysis in criminal justice research adds another element: relationships among the variables themselves.
3.   Thus, univariate analysis and subgroup comparisons focus on describing the *people* (or other units of analysis) under study, and bivariate analysis focuses on the *variables*.

B.   How do you read a percentage table?

1.   The comparison of subgroups, then, is essential in reading an explanatory bivariate table.
2.   We have used a convention called *percentage down* for constructing and presenting tables.
3.   This term means that you can add the percentages down each column to ❂ ❂ ❂   .
4.   You read this form of table ❂ ❂ ❂   .

C.   The direction of percentaging in tables is arbitrary, and some researchers prefer to percentage across.

1.   In reading a table that someone else has constructed, therefore, you need to find out in which manner ❂ ❂ ❂   .
2.   Usually that will be apparent in the labeling of the table or in the logic of the variables being analyzed.

D.   The steps involved in the construction of explanatory bivariate tables are as follows:

1.   The cases are divided into groups according to attributes of the ❂ ❂ ❂   .

2.   Each of these subgroups is then described in terms of attributes of the dependent variable.
3.   Finally, the table is ready by comparing the independent variable subgroups with one another in terms of a given attribute of the ❂ ❂ ❂   .

216

E. Tables such as those we've been examining are commonly called *contingency tables*: values of the dependent variable are contingent on values of the independent variable.

F. Certain guidelines should be followed in the presentation of most tabular data.

　　1. A table should have a heading or a title that succinctly describes what is contained in the table.
　　2. The original content of the variables should be clearly presented--in the table itself if at all possible or in the text with a paraphrase in the table.
　　3. The attributes of each variable should be ⦾ ⦾ ⦾　　　　　.
　　4. When percentages are reported in the table, the base on which they are computed should be indicated.
　　5. If any cases are omitted from the table because of missing data ("no answer," for example), their numbers should be indicated in the table.

G. By following these guidelines and by thinking carefully about the kinds of causal and descriptive relationships you want to examine, you will find that contingency tables can address many policy and research questions in criminal justice.

VI. *Multivariate Analysis*

A. A great deal of criminal justice researchers use multivariate techniques to ⦾ ⦾ ⦾

B. Multivariate tables may be constructed on the basis of a more complicated subgroup description by following essentially the same steps outlined previously for bivariate tables.

　　1. Instead of one independent variable and one dependent variable, however, we will have more than one independent variable.
　　2. Instead of explaining the dependent variable on the basis of a single independent variable, we'll seek an explanation through the use of more than one independent variable.

C. Just as subgroup comparisons can constitute a type of bivariate analysis, comparing values on some dependent variable across multiple subgroups is a type of multivariate analysis.

　　1. Multiple-subgroup comparisons are most frequently used to compare values for dependent variables measured at the ⦾ ⦾ ⦾　　　　.
　　2. Multiple-subgroup comparison can provide useful information about the relationship between more than one independent variable and dependent variables measured at the interval or ratio level.

VII.   *Measures of Association*

A.   Bivariate contingency tables offer one way to examine the association between
◐ ◐ ◐

1.   But sometimes contingency tables can be quite complex, presenting a number of different response categories for row and column variables.
2.   Nevertheless, a contingency table represents the association between two variables as a data matrix.
3.   But a variety of descriptive statistics permit the summarization of this data matrix.
4.   Selecting the appropriate measure depends initially on the nature of the two variables.

B.   Each measure of association we'll discuss is based on the same model--*proportionate reduction of error* (PRE). To see how this model works, let's assume that we asked you to guess respondents' attributes on a given variable: for example, whether they answered yes or no to a given questionnaire item.

1.   Let's first assume you know the overall distribution of responses in the total sample--say, 60 percent said yes and 40 percent said no. You would make the fewest errors in this process if you ◐ ◐ ◐

2.   Second, let's assume you also know the empirical relationship between the first variable and some other variable--say, <u>gender</u>. Now, each time we ask you to guess whether a respondent said yes or no, we'll tell you whether the respondent is a man or a woman. If the two variables are related, you should make fewer errors the second time.
3.   It is possible, therefore, to compute the PRE by knowing the relationship between the two variables: the greater the relationship, ◐ ◐ ◐

C.   If the two variables consist of nominal data (for example, <u>gender</u> marital status, race), lambda would be one appropriate measure.

1.   Lambda is based on your ability to guess values on one of the variables: the PRE achieved through knowledge of values on the other variables.
2.   Lambda represents the reduction in errors as a proportion of the errors that would have been made on the basis of the overall distribution.
3.   Lambda is only one of several measures of association appropriate to the analysis of two nominal variables.

D.   If the variables being related are ordinal (for example, occupational status or education), gamma is one appropriate measure of association.

1. Like lambda, gamma is based on your ability to guess values on one variable by knowing values on another.
2. Instead of guessing exact values, however, gamma is based on the ❂ ❂ ❂
3. For any given pair of cases, you guess that their original ranking on one variable will correspond (positively or negatively) to their ordinal ranking on the other.

E. Gamma is computed from two quantities: (l) the number of pairs having the same ranking on the two variables and (2) the number of pairs having the opposite ranking on the two variables.

    1. The pairs having the same ranking are computed as follows. The frequency of each cell in the table is multiplied by the sum of all cells appearing below and to the right of it--with all these products being summed.
    2. The pairs having the opposite ranking on the two variables are computed as follows. The frequency of each cell in the table is multiplied by the sum of all cells appearing below and to the left of it--with all these products being summed.

F. Gamma is computed from the numbers of same-ranked pairs and opposite-ranked pairs as follows:

$$\text{Gamma} = \frac{\text{same} - \text{opposite}}{\text{same} + \text{opposite}}$$

    1. Note that whereas values of lambda vary from 0 to 1, values of gamma vary from -1 to +1, representing the direction as well as the magnitude of the association.
    2. Because nominal variables have no ordinal structure, it makes no sense to speak of the direction of the relationship.

G. If interval or ratio variables (for example, age, income, number of arrests, and so forth) are being associated, one appropriate measure of association is *Pearson's product-moment correlation (r)*.

    1. Like both gamma and lambda, *r* is based on ❂ ❂ ❂
    2. For continuous interval or ratio variables, however, it is unlikely that you would be able to predict the precise value of the variable.
    3. But on the other hand, predicting only the ordinal arrangement of values on the two variables would not take advantage of the greater amount of information conveyed by an interval or ratio variable.

4. In a sense, r reflects how closely you can guess the value of one variable through your knowledge of the value of the other.
5. In the case of r, errors are measured in terms of the ⦿ ⦿ ⦿ .

H. We have referred to the general formula for describing the association between two variables: $Y = f(X)$.

I. Regression analysis is a method of determining the specific function relating Y to X: there are several forms of regression analysis.

1. The regression model can be seen most clearly in the case of a perfect linear association between two variables.
2. The linear regression model has important descriptive uses. The regression line offers a graphic picture of the association between X and Y, and the regression equation is an efficient form for summarizing that association.
3. To the extent that the regression equation correctly describes the general association between the two variables.

J. If you've ever studied geometry, you'll know that any straight line on a graph can be represented by an equation of the form $Y = a + bX$, where X and Y are values of the two variables.

1. In this equation, a equals the value of Y when X is 0, and b represents ⦿ ⦿ ⦿ .
2. If we know the values of a and b, we can calculate an estimate of Y for every value of X.
3. Regression analysis is a technique for establishing the regression equation representing the geometric line that comes closest to the distribution of points.
4. This equation is valuable both ⦿ ⦿ ⦿ .

K. To improve your guessing, you construct a regression line, stated in the form of a regression equation that permits the estimation of values on one variable from values on the other.

1. The general format for this equation is $Y' = a + b(X)$, and a and b are computed values, X is a given value on one variable, and Y' is the estimated value on the other.
2. The values of a and b are computed to minimize the differences between actual values of Y and the corresponding estimates (Y') based on ⦿ ⦿ ⦿ .

3.	The sum of squared differences between actual and estimated values of Y is called the *unexplained variation* because it represents errors that still exist even when estimates are based on known values of X.

4.	The *explained variation* is the ❂ ❂ ❂

L.	Dividing the explained variation by the total variation produces a measure of the proportionate reduction of error corresponding to the similar quantity in the computation of lambda.

◇	In the present case, this quantity is the correlation squared: r^2. Thus, if $r = .7$, then $r^2 = .49$, meaning that about half the variation has been explained.

M.	Often, criminal justice researchers find that a given dependent variable is affected simultaneously by several independent variables. *Multiple regression analysis* provides a means to analyzing such situations.

1.	Notice that in place of the single X variable in a linear regression (as described in the previous section, there are several Xs, and there are also several b's instead of just one.

2.	Also, the equation ends with a residual factor (e), which represents the variance in Y that is not completely accounted for by ❂ ❂ ❂

3.	The multiple-correlation coefficient is an indicator of the extent to which the three independent variables predict the dependent variable.

4.	This follows the same logic as the simple bivariate correlation discussed earlier, and it is traditionally reported as a capital R.

N.	The use of regression analysis for statistical inferences is based on the same assumptions made for correlational analysis: simple random sampling, the absence of nonsampling errors, and continuous interval data.

◇	Regression lines can be useful for interpolation (estimating cases lying between those observed), but they are less trustworthy when used for ❂ ❂ ❂

VIII.	*Inferential Statistics*

A.	Many criminal justice research projects involve the examinations of data collected from a sample drawn from a larger population.

1.	Researchers seldom if ever study samples just to describe the samples per se; in most instances, their ultimate purpose is to make assertions about the larger population from which the sample has been selected.

2. Frequently, then, you will wish to interpret your univariate and multivariate sample findings as ❿ ❿ ❿   .

IX. *Univariate Inferences*

A. The opening sections of this chapter dealt with methods of presenting univariate data. Each summary measure was intended as a method of describing the sample studied.

   ◇ This section addresses two univariate measures: percentages and means.

B. In the case of a percentage, the quantity

$$s = \sqrt{\frac{p \times q}{n}}$$

where *p* is a percentage, *q* equals *1 - p,* and *n* is the sample size, is called the *standard error.*

   1. As noted in Chapter 9, this quantity is very important in the estimation of sampling error.
   2. We may be 68 percent confident that the population figure falls within plus or minus one standard error of the sample figure, we may be 95 percent confident that it falls within plus or minus two standard errors, and we may be 99.9 percent confident that it falls within plus or minus three standard errors.

C. Any statement of sampling error, then, must contain two essential components:

   1. The *confidence level* (for example, 95 percent).
   2. The *confidence interval* (for example, 2.5 percent).

D. Recognize that we have moved beyond simply describing the sample into the realm of making estimates (inferences) about the larger population. In doing that, we must be wary of several assumptions.

   1. First, the sample must be drawn from the population about which ❿ ❿ ❿   .

   2. Second, the inferential statistics assume simple random sampling, which is virtually never the case in sample surveys.
   3. Third, inferential statistics are addressed to sampling error only; they do not take account of ❿ ❿ ❿   .

X.   *Tests of Statistical Significance*

A.   There is no scientific answer to the question of whether a given association between two variables is significant, strong, important, interesting, or worth reporting.

   1.   Perhaps the ultimate test of significance rests with your ability to persuade your audience (present and future) of the association's significance.
   2.   At the same time, a body of inferential statistics--called parametric tests of significance--can assist you in this regard.

B.   Recall that a sample statistic normally provides the best single estimate of the corresponding population parameter, but the statistic and the parameter seldom correspond precisely.

   1.   Thus, we report the probability that the parameter falls within a certain range (confidence interval).
   2.   The degree of uncertainty within the range is due ❂ ❂ ❂   .

XI.   *The Logic of Statistical Significance*

A.   The logic of statistical significance can be illustrated in a series of diagrams representing the selection of samples from a population. The elements in the logic we will illustrate are:

   1.   Assumptions regarding the *independence* of two variables in the population study.
   2.   Assumptions regarding the *representativeness* of samples selected through conventional probability sampling procedures.
   3.   The observed *joint distribution* of sample elements in terms of the two variables.

B.   The fundamental logic of tests of statistical significance, then, is this: faced with any discrepancy between the assumed independence of variables in a population and the observed distribution of sample elements, we may explain that discrepancy in either of two ways:

   1.   We may attribute it to ❂ ❂ ❂   .
   2.   We may reject the ❂ ❂ ❂   .
   3.   The logic and statistics associated with probability sampling methods offer guidance about the varying probabilities of varying degrees of unrepresentativeness (expressed as sampling error).
   4.   Most simply put, there is a high probability of a small degree of unrepresentativeness and a low probability of a large degree of unrepresentativeness.

C.   The *statistical significance* of a relationship observed in a set of sample data, then, is always expressed in terms of probabilities.

1.   Significant at the .05 level (p ≤ .05) simply means that the probability of a relationship as strong as the observed one being attributable to sampling error alone is no more than ◉◉◉   .

2.   Put somewhat differently, if two variables are independent of one another in the population, and if 100 probability samples were selected from that population, no more than 5 of those samples should provide a relationship as strong as the one that has been observed.

D.   There is, then, a corollary to confidence intervals in tests of significance, which represent the probability of the measured associations being due only to sampling error.

E.   This is called the **level of significance.**

1.   Like confidence intervals, levels of significance are derived from a logical model in which several samples are drawn from a given population.

2.   Three levels of significance are frequently used in research reports: .05, .01, and .001. These mean, respectively, that the chances of obtaining the measured association as a result of sampling error are no more that 5/100, 1/100, and 1/1,000.

XII.   *Chi Square*

A.   Chi square X^2 is a frequently used ◉◉◉   in criminal justice research.

1.   It is based on the **null hypothesis:** the assumption that ◉◉◉

2.   Given the observed distribution of values on the two separate variables, we compute the conjoint distribution that would be expected if there were no relationship between the two variables.

3.   The result of this operation is a set of expected frequencies for all the cells in the contingency table.

4.   We then compare this expected distribution with the distribution of cases actually found in the sample data, and we determine the probability that ◉◉◉   .

B.   Chi square is computed as follows.

1.   For each cell in the table, the researcher (1) subtracts the expected frequency for that cell from the observed frequency.

2.   Squares this quantity.

3.   Divides the squared difference by the expected frequency.
4.   This procedure is carried out for each cell in the tables, and the result are added together.
5.   The final sum is the value of chi square (12.70 in the example provided in the text).

C.   To determine the statistical significance of the observed relationship, we must use a standard set of chi-square values.

1.   That will require the computation of the *degrees of freedom.*
2.   For chi square, the degrees of freedom are computed as follows: The number of rows in the table of observed frequencies, minus one, is multiplied by the number of columns, minus one.

XIII.   *Cautions in Interpreting Statistical Significance*

A.   Tests of significance provide an ❂ ❂ ❂

      ◇   They assist us in ruling out associations that may not represent genuine relationships in the population under study.

B.   The researcher who uses or reads reports of significance tests should remain wary of certain dangers in their interpretation, however.

1.   First, we have been discussing tests of *statistical* significance; there are no objective tests of ❂ ❂ ❂   .
2.   Thus, we may be legitimately convinced that a given association is not due to sampling error, but we may be in the position of asserting without fear of contradiction that two variables are only slightly related to one another.
3.   Recall that sampling error is an inverse function of sample size; the larger the sample, the ❂ ❂ ❂   .
4.   Thus, a correlation of, say, .1 might well be significant (at a given level) if discovered in a large sample, whereas the same correlation between the same two variables would not be significant if found in a smaller sample.
5.   With small sample sizes, even moderately large differences might result from sampling error.

C.   You should not calculate statistical significance on relationships observed in data collected from ❂ ❂ ❂   .

D.   Tests of significance are based on the same sampling assumptions we used in the computation of confidence intervals. To the extent that these assumptions are not met by the actual sampling design, the tests of significance are not strictly legitimate.

225

Key Names and Terms

bivariate analysis
central tendency
contingency tables
degrees of freedom
descriptive statistics
deviation
dispersion
explained variation
frequency distributions
inferential statistics
median
mode
variance

multiple regression analysis
multivariate analysis
null hypothesis
Pearson's product-moment correlation
percentage
percentile
rates
regression analysis
standard error
skewed distributions
unexplained variation
univariate analysis

Multiple Choice Questions

1. The description of the associations between two variables is known as

   a. univariate analysis.
   b. marginal analysis.
   c. bivariate analysis.
   d. multivariate analysis.

2. Which of the following is an example of a measure of central tendency?

   a. mode.
   b. marginal.
   c. range.
   d. standard deviation.

3. Number of prior arrests is an example of which type of variable?

   a. discrete.
   b. continuous.
   c. continual.
   d. bivariate.

4. Dr. Hannan is studying the effect of media coverage of a particularly gruesome murder trial on attitudes toward capital punishment. She discovers that there is a relationship between length of exposure to graphic media coverage and feeling positively about capital punishment. However, she would like to control for the effect of gender. Which of the following would be most appropriate for her to use in order to discover whether this relationship exists? She should

    a.   calculate a measure of dispersion.
    b.   construct a bivariate contingency table.
    c.   compute Lambda.
    d.   use multivariate analysis.

5. Dr. Manzanares has found a rather complex relationship between two nominal variables. What is one appropriate measure of association which she might employ in order to summarize the relationship?

    a.   gamma.
    b.   lambda.
    c.   chi-square.
    d.   product-moment correlation.

6. Which of the following is a test of substantive significance?

    a.   chi-square.
    b.   lambda.
    c.   regression.
    d.   none of the above.

Use the following frequency distribution for the next three questions. (100 single mothers were asked: "How many children do you have?")

Number of children	Number of single mothers
1	5
2	20
3	35
4	25
5	12
6	3

7.   What is the mean number of children reported by the sample of single mothers?

    a.   3.50
    b.   3.28
    c.   3.00
    d.   3.25

8.   What is the modal number of children in the sample?

    a.   3.50
    b.   3.00
    c.   6.00
    d.   1.00

9.   What is the median number of children in the sample?

    a.   3.00
    b.   3.58
    c.   3.28
    d.   3.50

10.   Which of the following is not an assumption for regression analysis? (You may choose more than one response.)

    a.   ordinal level data
    b.   simple random sampling
    c.   the absence of nonsampling errors
    d.   nominal level data

11.   The number of traffic tickets given in one day is an example of which type of variable? (You may choose more than one response.)

    a.   ordinal
    b.   discrete
    c.   categorical
    d.   continuous

12.   Political affiliation (democrat, republican, libertarian, independent, other) is an example of which type of variable? (You may choose more than one response.)

    a.   discrete
    b.   ordinal
    c.   nominal
    d.   continuous

13. A researcher is interested in studying the effect of a number of neighborhood-related variables on the average number of 911 calls to the neighborhood each month. These independent variables include number of neighborhood residents on welfare, number of residents under age 15, and the median income of the neighborhood. The type of analysis most appropriate for this research is

    a. chi square analysis
    b. multiple regression analysis
    c. univariate analysis
    d. bivariate analysis

14. High dispersion of a variable could result in

    a. a low standard deviation
    b. small range
    c. very different values for the mean and median
    d. low variance

15. Dr. Eastman wishes to examine the relationship between median income of a census tract (independent variable) and the rate of burglaries reported to police in a census tract (dependent variable). She uses these variables in the regression equation $Y=a+bX$. Which symbol in the equation represents the median income?

    a. Y
    b. a
    c. b
    d. X

True/False Questions

1. The mean is a measure of association.

    a. true
    b. false

2. Percentiles are indicators which express both dispersion and grouping of cases.

    a. true
    b. false

3. When reading crosstabulated information, one should always read across the rows.

    a. true
    b. false

4.   If variables being related are ordinal, gamma is an appropriate measure of association.

      a.   true
      b.   false

5.   The statistical significance of a relationship is always expressed in terms of probabilities.

      a.   true
      b.   false

6.   There are objective tests of substantive significance.

      a.   true
      b.   false

7.   Statistical significance is the same as substantive significance.

      a.   true
      b.   false

8.   Comparing city size to murder rate would be an example of bivariate analysis

      a.   true
      b.   false

9.   Percentage should be computed to total 100 within categories of the independent variable

      a.   true
      b.   false

10.   Rates are computed to standardize the same measure, often for subgroup comparison.

      a.   true
      b.   false

Essay Questions

1. What is the difference between univariate and bivariate analysis? How is the focus of their description different? Briefly outline a criminological theory which can be tested through research. Provide an example of how both a univariate and bivariate analysis could be used to examine the validity of the theory selected.

2. Explain the differences between substantive and statistical significance. Describe research situations in which a relationship could be substantively significant, but not statistically significant. Also describe the opposite situation.

3. Dr. Ackerman's data analysis of the relationship between attitudes toward death and type of diet showed the following.

		Attitudes Toward Death	
		Pro	Anti
D I E T	Vegetarians	60%	60%
	Meat-Eaters	40%	40%
		(200)	(200)

Please answer the following questions

a. What is the relationship between attitudes toward death and diet?
b. Is the relationship statistically significant at the .05 level? At the .01 level? How would you determine this?